*For Matthew, Elizabeth, and Annie,*
*who helped to put magic into my life,*
*and Barbara,*
*who keeps it there*

# Magic Science

Other Titles of Interest by Jim Wiese

## Roller Coaster Science
50 Wet, Wacky, Wild, Dizzy Experiments
about Things Kids Like Best

## Rocket Science
50 Flying, Floating, Flipping, Spinning Gadgets
Kids Create Themselves

## Detective Science
40 Crime-Solving, Case-Breaking, Crook-Catching
Activities for Kids

## Spy Science
40 Secret-Sleuthing, Code-Cracking, Spy-Catching
Activities for Kids

## Cosmic Science
Over 40 Gravity-Defying, Earth-Orbiting, Space-Cruising
Activities for Kids

## Magic Science
50 Jaw-Dropping, Mind-Boggling, Head-Scratching
Activities for Kids

# Magic Science

## 50 Jaw-Dropping, Mind-Boggling, Head-Scratching Activities for Kids

### JIM WIESE

## JOHN WILEY & SONS, INC.

New York • Chichester • Weinheim • Brisbane • Singapore • Toronto

Copyright© 1998 by Jim Wiese.
Published by John Wiley & Sons, Inc.
Text design and production by Navta Associates, Inc.
Illustrations by Tina Cash-Walsh.

*Library of Congress Cataloging-in-Publication Data*
Wiese, Jim
    Magic science : 50 jaw-dropping, mind-boggling, head-scratching
activities for kids / Jim Wiese.
        p.    cm.
    Includes bibliographical references and index.
    Summary: Provides instructions for science projects and
experiments that can be performed as magic tricks and which require
materials readily found in the house or neighborhood.
    ISBN 0-471-18239-7 (pbk. : alk. paper)
    1. Science projects—Juvenile literature.   2. Science—
Experiments—Juvenile literature.   [1. Science projects.
2. Science—Experiments.   3. Experiments.]   I. Title.
Q182.3.W54   1998
507.8—dc21   97-29444

# Contents

# Introduction

Have you ever watched a magician perform a magic trick and wondered how it was done? Have you watched your science teacher do a science experiment and wondered the same thing? Sometimes it seems there's not much difference between magic and science. What are magic tricks anyway? Magic tricks are really just illusions. The magician knows the secret of how to do the trick. But to the audience, the trick looks like magic because the audience doesn't understand how the trick is done.

Many magic tricks are really just simple science experiments. The magician adds a few magic words and makes you believe that something supernatural and mysterious is happening. Actually, there's a scientific explanation for how the trick works that has nothing to do with the magic words.

So, if you're interested in magic and in understanding the science that makes many magic tricks work, you're going to love the activities in this book. They are all science projects and experiments, but with a wave of your hand and a few special words, your friends and family will believe you've made magic!

## How to Use This Book

This book is divided into chapters based on the general science subject areas of: matter, reactions, water, air, forces and energy, and magnetism and electricity. In each chapter are science projects and experiments that can be performed as magic tricks. Each project has a list of materials. You'll be able to find most of the materials needed around the house or at your neighborhood hardware or grocery store.

Each project is divided into two parts: **The Setup**, which tells you how to prepare the activity before your audience arrives, and **Magic Science Time!** which tells you how to perform the trick. Some of the projects have a section called **More Fun Stuff to Do** that tells you how to try different variations on the original activity. A **Magic Science Trick Tips** section gives hints on performing magic tricks for many of the projects. The **Effect** you want to achieve in the trick and a full **Explanation** are given at the end of each project. Words in **bold** type are defined in the text and in the Glossary at the back of the book.

## How to Do the Projects

- Read through the instructions once completely and collect all the equipment you'll need before you start the project.

- Keep a notebook. Write down what you do in each project and what happens.

- Follow the instructions carefully. *Do not attempt to do by yourself any steps that require the help of an adult.*

- If your project doesn't work properly the first time, try again or try doing it in a slightly different way. Experiments don't always work perfectly the first time.

## How to Be a Good Magician

In order to be a good magician, you'll need to master the four p's: props, preparation, practice, and performance.

*Props.* Props are the tools and equipment a magician uses, including a table, the items needed to do the trick, the magician's clothes, and a magic wand. You'll need to spend time making and decorating your props before you perform. Here are a few of the props every magician needs:

- *A magician's table.* Cover a table with a piece of decorated fabric, such as a large piece of black cloth decorated with tinfoil stars and moons. You can hide the rest of your props underneath it.

- *A backdrop* to go behind your stage. The backdrop also can be a large piece of black cloth decorated with tinfoil stars and moons. You can attach it to the wall with tape or thumbtacks. Ask permission before you stick anything to the wall.

- *The magician's clothes.* Decorate an old hat and vest with sequins or other shiny materials. Make crescent moons and stars out of tinfoil and sew them onto your outfit.

- *A magic wand.* Paint a stick black and attach streamers, a star, or a crescent moon to one end.

*Preparation.* Plan out which tricks you'll do in your act. Have some long tricks and some short tricks to make it more interesting.

*Practice.* Try every magic trick several times. Wait until you can do the tricks smoothly before you perform them for family or friends. All your movements should seem perfectly normal. Practice in front of a mirror until everything looks just right.

*Performance.* Add magic words like "abracadabra" or "presto-chango" to your routine to make it seem as if you're making magic happen. Tell jokes to keep your audience entertained. Remember to introduce yourself and your assistant (if you have one) to your audience, and to thank your audience for watching at the end. And don't forget to take a bow!

# USING THIS BOOK TO DO A SCIENCE FAIR PROJECT

Many of the activities in this book can serve as the starting point for a science fair project. After doing the experiment as it is written in the book, what questions come to mind? Some possible projects are suggested in the sections called More Fun Stuff to Do.

To begin your science fair project, first write down the problem you want to study and come up with a hypothesis. A **hypothesis** is an educated guess about the results of an experiment you are going to perform. The purpose of a hypothesis is to give a possible explanation of how something happens. For example, if you enjoyed the Milky Magic project, you might wonder if other kinds of milk, such as low-fat or skim milk, will work just as well as whole homogenized milk does. A hypothesis for this experiment could be that whole homogenized milk will work best.

To test your hypothesis, first create an experiment. In the Milky Magic activity, you might try the experiment three times, each time with a different kind of milk: whole homogenized, low-fat, and skim. Be sure to keep careful records of your experiment. Next, analyze the data you recorded. In some projects, you could draw pictures or create a chart or graph to show the results of each experiment. Finally, come up with a conclusion that shows how your results prove or disprove your hypothesis.

This process is called the **scientific method**. When following the scientific method, you begin with a hypothesis, test it with an experiment, analyze the results, and form a conclusion.

## A WORD OF WARNING

Some science experiments and magic tricks can be dangerous. *Ask an adult to help you with projects that call for adult help, such as those that involve matches, knives, or other dangerous materials.* Don't forget to ask an adult's permission to use household items, and put away your equipment and clean up your work area when you have finished. Good scientists and magicians are careful and avoid accidents.

# The Magic of Matter

## Solid Illusions

**C**hemistry is the science that studies **matter**, which is anything that has mass and occupies space. All matter is made up of tiny particles called **atoms**, and atoms bond or link together to form **molecules**.

There are three states of matter: solid, liquid, and gas. In solids, particles (atoms and molecules) are packed tightly together. They don't move around, they only vibrate in place, which is why solids have shapes that don't easily change.

Particles in liquids attract each other but they also slide around past each other. Liquids have a fixed **volume** (the amount of space occupied by a substance), but they change shape.

Particles in gases are far apart from one another and move around very quickly. This is why gases, like air, have no definite shape or volume.

Most substances exist in all three states. For example, water exists as solid ice, liquid water, and gaseous steam. In all forms, matter can be amazing. To learn more marvelous matter magic tricks, try the activities in this chapter.

## PROJECT

# Floating Eggs

*Sometimes a magician seems to make things float in air. In this project you won't make things float in air, but you will make an egg float in water.*

### MATERIALS

quart (liter) jar
tap water
scissors
ruler
masking tape
½ cup (125 ml) salt
felt-tip pen
uncooked egg
large spoon

## THE SETUP

1. Fill the jar half full of water.

2. Cut a 3-inch (7.5-cm) piece of tape and stick it to the outside of the salt container. Use the pen to write on the tape, "Magic Swimming Powder."

3. Place the egg and spoon on the table in easy reach.

## MAGIC SCIENCE TIME!

1. Tell your audience, "I am going to teach an egg how to swim."

2. Begin by showing the audience that the egg doesn't know how to swim by placing the egg in the jar filled with tap water. The egg should sink. With the spoon, quickly remove the egg from the jar, saying, "I don't want the egg to drown!"

3. Give the egg a few verbal swimming lessons. For example, say "Egg, take a deep breath before jumping in the water."

4. Tell the audience that to help the egg become a good swimmer, you need to add magic swimming powder to the water to help it swim.

5. Pour the salt in the water and stir with the spoon. Say a few magic words while you mix the salt into the water, such as "Magic powder, this we beg, make this water hold up an egg!"

6. Place the egg in the water.

## MAGIC SCIENCE TRICK TIPS

Add a few jokes to this magic trick. For example, you can say that this trick is very "eggciting," and that the egg that can swim is an "eggcellent" student in swimming class.

Do this trick to show that eggs can "read." Use a crayon to write "sink" on one egg and "swim" on another. Take two identical jars, and fill one half-full with tap water and the other half full with salt water.

Tell the audience that your eggs can read what you have written on them and will do what they are told. Place the egg marked "sink" in the tap water and the egg marked "swim" in the salt water. Your audience will be amazed as each egg does what is written on it.

### EFFECT

The egg sinks in tap water but floats in the salt water.

### EXPLANATION

Like the eggs, all matter floats or sinks depending on its density. **Density** is a physical property of matter. Density is used to compare two substances that have equal volume (occupy the same amount of space), but have unequal masses (contain different amounts of matter). An object with more mass per volume is more dense than an object with less mass per volume. Less dense substances float on more dense substances. The egg floats in salt water because the egg is less dense than the salt water. However, the egg is more dense than tap water, so it sinks.

Salt water is a **solution** that contains both salt and water. A solution occurs when a solid is dissolved in a liquid. When salt dissolves in water, the mass of the solution is greater than the mass of the water by itself for the same volume. The salt water is more dense.

You can feel density in action when you swim in the ocean. It's easier to float in the salt water of an ocean than in the fresh water of a pool or lake.

# 2 Density Tower

*In the previous trick, you made an egg float on water. This activity will make objects seem suspended in liquids.*

## MATERIALS

tall, narrow glass container, for example a clear, empty 2-cup (500-ml) olive jar

¼ cup (65 ml) corn syrup or honey

food coloring, any color

¼ cup (65 ml) tap water

¼ cup (65 ml) vegetable oil

¼ cup (65 ml) rubbing alcohol

small objects, such as a cork, a grape, a nut, a piece of dried pasta, a rubber ball, a cherry tomato, a small plastic object, a metal bolt

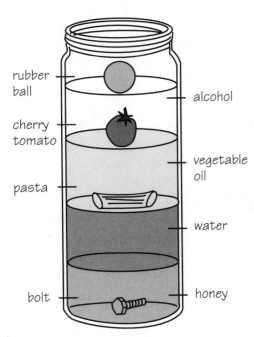

rubber ball — alcohol

cherry tomato — vegetable oil

pasta — water

bolt — honey

## THE SETUP

1. Carefully pour the honey into the container until the container is one-quarter full.

2. Add a few drops of food coloring to the water. Pour the water into the container until the container is half full. Note: As you add each liquid, pour it very carefully so that it does not disturb the previous layer.

3. Slowly pour the same amount of vegetable oil into the container.

4. Add enough rubbing alcohol to fill the container.

## MAGIC SCIENCE TIME!

1. Tell the audience that you are going to make several objects float. The audience may say that seems easy. Then tell them that you are going to make things float at different levels in the liquids.

2. Place the small objects in the container by gently placing them one at a time on the top of the liquid layers.

3. Let the audience observe what happens.

## EFFECT

The different objects float at different levels in the liquid. Some seem suspended in the middle of the liquid tower.

## EXPLANATION

This trick works because substances float or sink depending on their densities. Less dense substances float on more dense substances.

Alcohol floats on vegetable oil because it is less dense than oil. Vegetable oil floats on water because it is less dense than water. Water floats on honey and corn syrup because it is less dense than either honey or corn syrup.

When you drop the objects into the container, they sink or float depending on their density and the density of the liquid layers. A bolt has a higher density than any of the liquids so it sinks to the bottom. A piece of pasta has a higher density than alcohol, vegetable oil, or water but a lower density than honey, so it floats on the honey. A rubber ball is less dense than all of the liquids, so it floats on the surface of the alcohol.

## PROJECT 3

# Restless Raisins

*It's easy to make an object move if you push it with your hand. But how can you make raisins move without touching them? Try this activity to find out one way.*

## MATERIALS

cold can of ginger ale
drinking glass
6 raisins

## THE SETUP

1. Place the materials on the table.

2. Open the can and pour the ginger ale into the glass.

## MAGIC SCIENCE TIME!

1. Tell the audience, "I have some raisins that have had trouble sleeping lately. They are very restless and can't stop moving."

2. Place the raisins in the ginger ale.

3. Wait a few moments and watch what happens.

# MORE FUN STUFF TO DO

This activity can also be done using small pieces of spaghetti instead of raisins. Break spaghetti into ½-inch (1.25-cm) pieces and place them in the ginger ale.

## EFFECT

After a few minutes, the raisins begin to move up and down in the liquid.

## EXPLANATION

This effect occurs because the can of ginger ale contains a gas called carbon dioxide. Carbon dioxide gas has been dissolved in the ginger ale under pressure. When you open the can of ginger ale and pour it into the glass, the carbon dioxide gas is released. Carbon dioxide gas is less dense than the rest of the soda, so bubbles of carbon dioxide rise to the surface of the soda.

When you add the raisins to the ginger ale, carbon dioxide bubbles collect on the surface of each raisin. These bubbles combined with the raisins make the raisin less dense than the ginger ale. The bubble-covered raisins float to the surface of the ginger ale. At the surface the carbon dioxide bubbles break, and the raisins once again become more dense than the ginger ale. The bubble-free raisins sink back to the bottom of the glass. On the bottom of the glass, the carbon dioxide bubbles collect on the surface of the raisins again and the trip starts all over. This process will occur as long as the ginger ale continues to release enough carbon dioxide. After a short time, the ginger ale will stop releasing carbon dioxide and the process will stop.

# PROJECT 4 Magic Seesaw

*Magicians can sometimes make it seem as if there are invisible people helping them perform their magic. Learn how in this activity.*

***Note: This activity requires adult help.***

## MATERIALS

paring knife (to be used only by adult helper)
10-inch (25-cm) candle
ruler

2 straight pins

two tall drinking glasses

two saucers

matches (to be used only by adult helper)

adult helper

## THE SETUP

1. Have your adult helper use the knife to cut away about ½ inch (1.25 cm) of the wax from the bottom of the candle. The bottom should look like the top with the candlewick sticking out.

2. Use the ruler to find the center of the candle as accurately as possible. Make a small mark in the center with your fingernail.

3. Push one pin into each side of the center of the candle.

4. Rest the pins on the rims of the two glasses. The candle should balance. If one end tips lower than the other, ask your adult helper to trim a small amount of wax off that end until the candle balances horizontally (sideways). When balanced, the candle will rock back and forth very easily, like a seesaw.

## MAGIC SCIENCE TIME!

1. Tell the audience, "There is magic in the air. Two very small and invisible magic helpers are going to help me do this trick. These two helpers like to play, especially on the seesaw."

2. Place the candle-glass setup on the table. Say to your invisible helpers, "Come magic helpers, come to play on the seesaw I made for you." When nothing happens, tell the audience that the helpers are shy, in spite of being invisible, and need a place to hide.

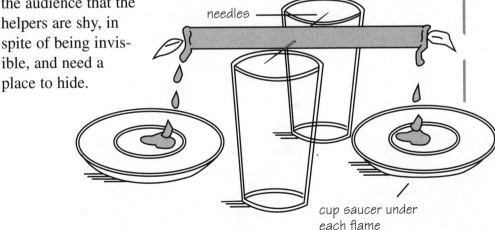

needles

cup saucer under each flame

3. Place one saucer under each end of the candle.

4. Have your adult helper use the matches to light each end of the candle. Tell the audience that your invisible helpers can now hide in the flame and play on the seesaw. Watch what happens. (Remember to blow out the candles when you've finished.)

## EFFECT

The candle rocks up and down like a seesaw.

## EXPLANATION

When you light a candle, the heat from the flame causes the particles in the candle wax to vibrate more and more. The particles break free from their fixed positions and move freely. The solid wax melts and turns into liquid wax.

In this activity, the end of the candle that your helper lights first begins to melt first. The liquid wax drips off of the rest of the candle onto the saucer. That first end of the candle becomes lighter and rises up. On the opposite end of the candle, the flame tilts nearer the wax on that end and it begins to melt faster. As the second end loses more liquid wax, it becomes lighter and rises. This process continues, causing the candle to rock back and forth.

## PROJECT 5

# What Is It?

*Magicians can make things change form before your eyes. But do they really change? Try this activity to find out.*

## MATERIALS

¼ cup (50 ml) cornstarch

clear plastic cup

¼ cup (50 ml) tap water

spoon

helper

## THE SETUP

1. Put the cornstarch in the cup.

2. Add the tap water, a little at a time, to the cornstarch. Stir the mixture with the spoon. Note: Be careful not to add too much water. The mixture should be very thick.

3. Put the cup in the middle of the table.

## MAGIC SCIENCE TIME!

1. Show the audience the white liquid in the cup. Tell them that you are going to make it turn into a solid and then back into a liquid. Ask for a volunteer to be your helper.

2. Pour about a tablespoon (15 ml) of the white liquid into one of your helper's hands. The liquid will pour very easily from the cup.

3. Have your helper touch the liquid with a finger of his or her other hand, and then remove the finger. Ask your helper to explain to the audience what happened.

## EFFECT

When your helper touches the cornstarch mixture it instantly turns hard. It then turns back into a liquid when the finger is removed.

## EXPLANATION

Matter takes the form of solid, liquid, or gas. However, solids, liquids and gases can be mixed together in interesting ways. When one substance dissolves or disappears completely into another, the result is called a solution. The cornstarch and water mixture is not a solution, however. It is a slightly different kind of mixture called a **colloid**. A colloid is a mixture of tiny particles of one substance scattered evenly throughout another. In this case, the cornstarch particles are scattered evenly throughout the water.

Colloids can change form under pressure. In this activity, when the mixture is in the cup, it appears to be a liquid. But when your helper touches the solution, the touch puts pressure on the mixture. The pressure forces the cornstarch particles together and the mixture becomes solid. When the pressure is released, the mixture returns to its original liquid form.

## PROJECT
# 6 Leak Sealer

*What would happen if you put water in a container that has a hole in it? The water would pour out, right? But that's not always the case, as you'll see in this activity.*

### MATERIALS
polyethylene plastic bag (Many grocery stores use these in their
   produce sections.)
pitcher of tap water
rubber band
sharp pencil
plastic tub or baking pan

### THE SETUP
1. Put water into the plastic bag to make sure that there are no holes in it. You should be able to fill the bag half full with water without it leaking.

2. Empty the bag and allow it to dry.

3. Place bag, pitcher of water, rubber band, pencil, and plastic tub on the table in front of you.

# MAGIC SCIENCE TIME!

1. Tell the audience, "I have a special magic bag that won't leak, even when I puncture it with a pencil."

2. Pour water into the plastic bag until it is half full.

3. Twist the top closed, removing most of the air in the bag, and seal it with the rubber band.

small amount of air

4. Hold the bag over the plastic tub or baking pan, holding the top of the bag with one hand. With the other hand, stab the pencil into the bottom half of the bag so that it goes in one side and out the other. Leave the pencil in place. What happens?

PRODUCE

# MAGIC SCIENCE TRICK TIPS

To make this trick even more spectacular, stab two or three pencils into the water-filled plastic bag.

# EFFECT

In spite of the two pencil-sized holes in the bag, it doesn't leak water.

# EXPLANATION

Plastic is a remarkable and useful material. It can be manufactured in several ways and can be shaped into virtually any form. Plastic is made of **polymers**. A polymer is a long chain of molecules joined together with chemical bonds. Plastic polymer chains can branch and join to chains next to them, making the plastic stronger.

One molecule that can be used to make plastics is ethylene. When ethylene molecules are joined together, they form **polyethylene plastic**, used to make plastic bags. Polyethylene plastic melts when heated. It also has a peculiar property. When torn, its molecules shrink together. When you puncture the bag with the pencil, the polyethylene plastic shrinks around the opening and closes off the hole.

Other materials have this property. This same peculiar property is used to make tires that do not go flat even when punctured by a nail.

# PROJECT 7 Pop It!

*Have you ever seen a magician stick a sharp object through a balloon without making it pop? Try this activity to learn how you can do it yourself.*

## MATERIALS

bamboo skewer
petroleum jelly or vegetable oil
2 balloons
helper

## THE SETUP

1. Coat the bamboo skewer with petroleum jelly or vegetable oil.

2. Place the materials on the table in front of you.

## MAGIC SCIENCE TIME!

1. Ask a member of the audience to be your helper.

2. Have your helper blow up one of the balloons and tie the end in a knot. Make sure that the balloon is blown up completely.

3. Ask your helper to take the skewer and stick it through the balloon without popping it. He or she will not be able to do it.

4. Blow up the second balloon to full size, but don't make a knot. Let some air out of the balloon to reduce the size of the balloon by about a third. (The balloon should be about two-thirds of the size it is when completely blown up.) Tie the end of the balloon in a knot.

5. Place the sharp tip of the skewer on the end of the balloon opposite the knot.

6. Spin the skewer by rotating it back and forth between your finger. Slowly apply pressure to the skewer while continuing to spin it until the tip of the skewer pierces the balloon's surface without popping it.

7. Continue to slowly push and spin the skewer through the balloon until the sharp tip reaches the opposite side of the balloon near the knot.

8. Keep applying pressure while spinning the skewer until the tip of the skewer pierces the balloon surface on the opposite side, without popping the balloon.

## MAGIC SCIENCE TRICK TIPS

This trick is difficult to do the first time. You'll probably need to practice it several times before trying it in front of an audience. You may need to add more petroleum jelly or vegetable oil to the skewer to make sure it doesn't burst the balloon.

end of balloon opposite knot

You can also try this trick by placing a small piece of clear tape on opposite sides of the balloon. Poke the skewer through the taped areas of the balloon.

## MORE FUN STUFF TO DO

Do all types of balloons work equally well for this trick? Try several different types of balloons to see which work best.

## EFFECT

The skewer passes completely through the balloon without the balloon popping.

# EXPLANATION

Balloons are made of rubber. You are able to pierce the balloon without it bursting because of the unique composition of rubber.

Rubber is made of molecules in long chains. These long chains of molecules are linked together crosswise, similar to a screen on a screen door, to create the balloon. This gives the balloon its stretchy consistency. When your helper quickly pierces the balloon, the chains break apart and the balloon bursts. However, when you very slowly pierce the balloon, the chains of molecules push apart slightly, making space for the skewer to pass through.

You make it easier for the skewer to pass between the chains when you blow up the balloon and then reduce its volume. Blowing up the balloon completely and then releasing air weakens the chains of molecules in some places. This allows the skewer to pass through the balloon more easily. The petroleum jelly also helps by serving as a **lubricant**, which is a filmlike substance that reduces **friction** (a force that opposes motion) between solid surfaces. The jelly reduces the friction between the skewer and the balloon, allowing the skewer to pass more easily through the balloon.

# The Magic of Reactions

## Mix-It-Up Stunts

A **chemical** is any substance that can change when combined with another substance. Mixing two chemicals together often results in a chemical reaction. A **chemical reaction** sounds mysterious, but it's actually just a change in matter in which substances break apart to produce one or more new substances. When chemical reactions occur, they sometimes seem like magic. A magician uses chemistry and chemical reactions to make the colors of liquids change, make liquids turn into solids, and create many other strange and wonderful illusions.

To learn how chemical reactions can be used in some amazing magic tricks, try the activities in this chapter.

**PROJECT**

# 1   Where's the Water?

*Try this activity to make water seem to disappear.*

## MATERIALS

several sheets of newspaper
scissors
disposable diaper
3 identical paper cups
pitcher of tap water

## THE SETUP

1. Spread the newspaper over your work area.

2. Use the scissors to cut the diaper in half the short way so that you can see inside it.

3. Take the diaper apart and remove the middle layer of cotton. Examine it closely. What do you see? How is this layer made?

4. Take the cotton layer and shake it vigorously back and forth over the newspaper. Small particles should come out of the cotton layer.

**5.** Put the particles into one of the paper cups.

## MAGIC SCIENCE TIME!

**1.** Tell your audience that you are going to make some water disappear. Quickly show them that the cups are empty. (*Quickly* is the key word. You don't want to let them see the particles in the bottom of the cup.)

**2.** Pour a small amount of water into one of the two empty cups. Switch the three cups around quickly, say a few magic words, then ask someone in the audience to guess which cup has the water. The person should be able to pick the right cup.

**3.** Say, "You are correct. I must have used the wrong magic words." Pour the water from the first cup into the cup with the particles.

**4.** Say some different magic words while you switch the three cups around quickly again. Then ask someone else which cup has the water.

**5.** The person should answer correctly. This time, after the person answers, turn the cup upside down. What happens?

## MAGIC SCIENCE TRICK TIP

Add some humor to your magic act to make it more entertaining. When the audience member picks the right cup in Step 2, pretend to be shocked that the magic trick didn't work. Tell the audience that you must have used the wrong magic words. Take out a prop book titled, "Magic Words for All Occasions." (You can make this prop book by covering any other book with white paper and writing the suggested title on it.) Pretend to pick out a new word or words, then proceed with Step 3.

## EFFECT

When you turn over the cup containing the water and the particles, no water pours out. The water seems to have disappeared.

## EXPLANATION

The particles in the cotton layer of the diaper are a chemical called polysodium acrylate. When you mix the water with the particles, a chemical reaction occurs. The mixture of the particles and water forms a new substance, a sticky gel, that does not pour out of the cup.

The particles from the diaper have a strong **hygroscopic** nature, which means that they can **absorb** (take in) and hold water. Some hygroscopic chemicals can absorb and hold over 50 times their weight in water. Diaper manufacturers add the hygroscopic chemical to diapers to hold moisture and help keep babies dry. You can also purchase polysodium acrylate from magic stores under the name Water Slush.

## PROJECT 2 Milky Magic

*You've probably seen magicians make beautiful flowers seem to appear out of thin air. Try this activity to make beautiful flowing patterns out of ordinary household materials.*

### MATERIALS

1 cup (250 ml) whole homogenized milk
pie plate
blue food coloring
1 tablespoon (15 ml) liquid Palmolive dish soap

### THE SETUP

Place all the materials on your table.

### MAGIC SCIENCE TIME!

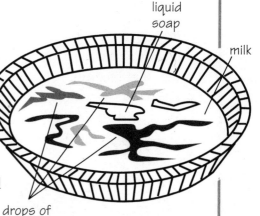

liquid soap

milk

drops of food coloring

1. Tell the crowd that you are going to make beautiful swirls in ordinary milk.

2. Pour the milk into the pie plate. It should be about ½-inch (1.25-cm) deep.

3. Add drops of food coloring to several places on the surface of the milk.

4. Add the dish soap to the center of the milk.

5. Wait a few moments, then watch what happens.

Try putting different colors of food coloring in the milk. When the colors mix, you will get new colors. For example, if you use red and yellow food coloring, the two colors will mix to make orange.

### EFFECT

The soap causes the milk and food coloring to mix, creating swirls of colors in the milk. This continues for several minutes.

### EXPLANATION

The milk in this activity is **homogenized**, which means that the fat in it has been made very fine and spread evenly throughout the milk. When you add the food coloring to the milk, at first nothing happens. The food coloring will remain where you put it. However, when you add the soap, the soap begins to spread out. Soap particles are **polar molecules**; one end of the particle (molecule) has a positive charge and the other end of the particle has a negative charge. Since opposite charges are attracted to one another, the positive end of the soap particle is attracted to negatively charged parts of the fat particles in the milk. The soap particles link to the fat particles in the milk and begin to spread the fat particles around. As the fat particles move, they move the food coloring as well. This movement causes the food coloring to mix with the white milk, resulting in swirls of colors.

## PROJECT 3  Magic Writing

*Try this activity to make an invisible message suddenly appear.*

## MATERIALS

¼ cup (65 ml) lemon juice

small jar

cotton swab

sheet of white paper

lamp with light bulb

## THE SETUP

1. Put the lemon juice into the small jar.

2. Dip the cotton swab into the lemon juice. Use the swab to write a message on the sheet of white paper such as, "Magic Act Tonight!"

3. Allow the message to dry. You should not be able to see the message after it has dried.

## MAGIC SCIENCE TIME!

1. Tell the audience, "I have written an invisible message on a piece of paper." Hold up the paper and say, "With special magic words, I will reveal the secret message."

2. Remove the lamp shade from the lamp and turn it on.

3. Hold the message close behind the light bulb and say your magic words. Watch what happens.

## MORE FUN STUFF TO DO

Try other liquids for this activity, such as orange juice or vinegar. Do they also work?

## EFFECT

Lemon juice is very light colored and is difficult to see after it has dried. However, when you hold the paper close to the light bulb, the heat from the bulb turns the lemon juice brown, and the hidden message appears!

## EXPLANATION

Fruit juices, such as lemon juice, and many other liquids, such as milk and soda, contain carbon atoms. In the lemon juice, these carbon atoms are linked, or bonded, to other atoms to form carbon-containing molecules.

These carbon-containing molecules have almost no color when dissolved in liquid. However, when these liquids are heated, a chemical reaction occurs. The carbon-containing molecules break apart and produce, among other substances, the element carbon. (An **element** is a substance that cannot be further broken down chemically.) Carbon is an element made up of carbon atoms that are found in all living matter. Carbon is black or brown in color, which is why the lemon juice turns brown when heated. Carbon also appears when you toast a piece of bread, which is why toast turns dark brown or black when burned.

# PROJECT 4 Starchy Starts

*Here's another way to make a magic message appear.*

## MATERIALS

several sheets of newspaper

2 sheets of plain white paper

scissors

spray starch

2 teaspoons (10 ml) tincture of iodine solution

   *CAUTION: Avoid getting this on your hands. It can stain.*

1 cup (250 ml) water

empty spray bottle

## THE SETUP

1. Cover your work area with newspaper.

2. Using one sheet of white paper, cut out letters to spell a secret message, such as "Magic Show Tonight!"

3. Place the second sheet of white paper on the newspaper. With the cut-out letters, spell out the message on the second sheet of paper.

4. Spray the sheet of paper and letters with the spray starch.

5. Remove the cut-out letters. Allow the bottom sheet to dry. This should take about 15 minutes, depending on the amount of spray starch you used. The message should be invisible.

6. Combine the tincture of iodine with the water in the spray bottle. Shake the bottle to mix the solution.

## MAGIC SCIENCE TIME!

1. Tell the audience that you have an invisible magic message on the paper. With the correct magic words, the message will appear.

2. Tape the paper to the wall, with the message facing out, and spray it with the water and iodine solution.

## Magic Science Trick Tips

This is an excellent magic trick to use to start your magic show. It is always a good idea to open your show with a trick that the audience will have trouble figuring out.

Try writing your magic message on an extra large sheet of paper. The words, "Magic Show Tonight!" will tell the audience that they are in for a great time.

## MORE FUN STUFF TO DO

You can create pictures to go along with your written messages. Cut out a shape, such as a snowflake, a crescent moon, or a star. Place the shape on the paper with the cut-out letters before spraying them with the starch spray.

## Effect

When you spray the paper with the iodine solution, your message appears as white letters on a purple background.

## Explanation

The starch you spray on the letters and paper is made up of molecules of sugar linked together in a long chain. The iodine you use to make the message appear is an element made up of iodine molecules. When the iodine solution hits the part of the paper that has the starch on it, a chemical reaction occurs. The sugar molecules and the iodine molecules combine to form complex starch-iodine molecules that are purple in color.

The part of the paper underneath the letters was protected from the starch spray, so it remains white. The rest of the paper, where the starch was sprayed, turns a light purple due to the chemical reaction of the starch with the iodine spray.

# Make It Pink

*Magicians often seem to make one substance turn into another. Is that really possible? Try this activity to learn how to change "water" into "pink lemonade."*

## MATERIALS

¼ cup (65 ml) rubbing alcohol (isopropyl alcohol)

glass jar

2 Ex-Lax chewing gum tablets

spoon

two drinking glasses

1 cup (250 ml) tap water

5 teaspoons (25 ml) ammonia

**CAUTION: Do not drink any of the liquids in the experiment.**

## THE SETUP

1. Pour the alcohol into the glass jar. Add the chewing gum tablets. Set the jar aside overnight. Use the spoon to stir the mixture the next morning.

2. Pour one teaspoon (5 ml) of the mixture from the jar into the first drinking glass. Add ½ cup (125 ml) of tap water to the mixture.

3. Pour the ammonia into the second glass. **CAUTION: Be careful not to spill any ammonia on your hands.** Add ½ cup (125 ml) of tap water to the ammonia.

## MAGIC SCIENCE TIME!

1. Tell your audience that you are going to turn the two glasses of water in front of you into pink lemonade.

2. Say a few magic words over the glasses, then pour the contents of the second glass into the first. Watch what happens!

## MAGIC SCIENCE TRICK TIP

Whenever you perform a magic trick, be sure to make a bow. This will signal the audience to clap for your performance.

## EFFECT

Well, you don't *really* make pink lemonade, but when you mix the two clear liquids together they turn pink.

## EXPLANATION

Ex-Lax and many other laxatives contain a chemical called phenolphthalein. Phenolphthalein dissolves in alcohol. When you place the laxative gum in the alcohol, it dissolves, forming a clear solution.

Phenolphthalein is also a **chemical indicator**. A chemical indicator is a chemical that changes color when mixed with certain substances called acids or bases. (An **acid** is a type of chemical that reacts with a base to form a salt and water. A **base** is a type of chemical that reacts with an acid to form a salt and water.)

The phenolphthalein and alcohol solution is **neutral**, which means it is neither an acid nor a base. Phenolphthalein is clear when mixed with an acid or neutral substance. However, it turns pink when mixed with a base. Ammonia is a base. So, when you add the ammonia to the phenolphthalein-and-alcohol solution, the solution turns pink.

# 6 Make It Clear

*In the previous activity, you made "water" appear to turn into "pink lemonade." In this activity, try it in reverse.*

## MATERIALS

¼ cup (65 ml) rubbing alcohol (isopropyl alcohol)

glass jar

2 Ex-Lax chewing gum tablets

drinking glass

½ cup (125 ml) tap water

spoon

powdered drain cleaner (without bleach)

1 Alka-Seltzer tablet

**CAUTION: Do not drink any of the liquids in the experiment.**

## THE SETUP

1. Pour the alcohol into the glass jar. Add the chewing gum tablets. Set the jar aside overnight. Use the spoon to stir the mixture in the morning.

2. Pour one teaspoon (5 ml) of the liquid from the jar into the glass. Add ½ cup (125 ml) of tap water. Stir the mixture again.

## MAGIC SCIENCE TIME!

1. Tell your audience that you are going to turn the glass of water in front of you into pink lemonade.

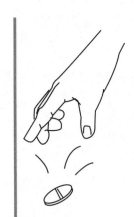

2. Say a few magic words over the solution. Use the spoon to add a few grains of "magic powder" (powdered drain cleaner) to the solution. What happens?

3. After the solution has changed color, tell your audience, "Pink lemonade always gives me a stomachache." Add the Alka-Seltzer tablet to the solution. What happens this time?

## EFFECT

When you add a few grains of powdered drain cleaner to laxative-and-alcohol solution, the solution turns pink. When you add the Alka-Seltzer, the solution turns clear again.

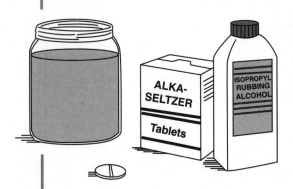

## EXPLANATION

As you learned in the last activity, the phenolphthalein in the laxative gum is a chemical indicator. Phenolphthalein is clear when mixed with acid or neutral substances, and pink when mixed with bases. Powdered drain cleaner is a base. When you add drain cleaner to the phenolphthalein-and-alcohol solution, the solution turns pink.

Alka-Seltzer dissolved in water releases a chemical called carbonic acid. Carbonic acid is a weak acid, commonly found in soda, that forms when carbon dioxide gas mixes with water. When an acid and base are mixed together, they **neutralize** each other, which means they cancel each other out. They form a neutral solution which is neither an acid nor a base. So when you mix carbonic acid from the Alka Seltzer with the basic drain cleaner, the acid and the base neutralize each other to form a neutral solution. Phenolphthalein is clear when mixed with a neutral solution, so the solution turns clear.

# The Magic of Water

## Liquid Tricks

ater covers about two-thirds of the surface of the Earth. People are about 65 percent water and a watermelon is more than 90 percent water. People need water to drink, as do most animals. Plants need water in the soil. Water is necessary for life as we know it to exist. For that reason alone, it seems magical.

But water is special for other reasons as well. Water molecules are made of two atoms of hydrogen and one atom of oxygen. This gives it a chemical formula of $H_2O$. Water can be found in all three states of matter in everyday life, and it is constantly changing forms. Liquid water **evaporates**, meaning it changes from liquid to gas. The gas form of water is **water vapor**. Water vapor **condenses**, or changes from gas to liquid. When water is heated to 212°F (100°C), it boils and changes into hot water vapor called **steam**. At 32°F (0°C) water freezes and changes into solid ice.

Try some of the "liquid tricks" in this chapter to learn more about water and some of its other special properties.

## PROJECT

# Rock Solid

*Sometimes what you think will happen does not. Try this trick to fool your friends.*

*Note: This activity requires adult help.*

### MATERIALS

2 cups (250 ml) water in plastic cups
microwave oven
oven mitts
adult helper

### THE SETUP

1. Place one cup of water in the freezer for at least two days to make sure that the water in the cup is frozen solid.

2. Place both cups of water on the table.

# MAGIC SCIENCE TIME!

1. Pick an adult from the audience to be your helper.

2. Ask the audience: "What do you think will happen when I put both a cup of water and an equal-sized block of ice in a microwave for two minutes?" They will probably tell you that the ice will melt and the water will get hotter.

3. Place both cups in the microwave.

4. Set the microwave to HI for 2 minutes, then immediately start the microwave.

5. After two minutes, have your adult helper put on the oven mitts and remove both cups from the microwave.

# MAGIC SCIENCE TRICK TIPS

The cup of ice must be frozen solid for this trick to work best. Use a chest freezer if you have one, because they are usually colder than the freezer compartment in a refrigerator.

## EFFECT

The cup of ice will remain frozen while the cup of water will be almost boiling.

## EXPLANATION

When water is in its solid state—ice—the water molecules are packed tightly together. These tightly packed molecules vibrate. When water is in its liquid state, the water molecules not only vibrate, but also rotate or spin around. As the water gets warmer, the molecules move around even more and start bumping into each other.

A microwave heats food by speeding up the rotation and motion of molecules in the food. However, a microwave has little effect on molecules that can only vibrate. So when both the ice and the water are in the microwave, the microwave increases the temperature of the water but has almost no effect on the ice.

If you put ice in a microwave for a longer period of time, it will melt. The ice will start to melt and turn to water not because of the microwave, but because of the heat in the room. Since water is affected by a microwave, the small amounts of melted water will be heated and melt the ice next to it. This process continues and eventually the ice in the microwave will melt.

This is how a microwave can be used to defrost frozen food. The microwave is set to a lower temperature. The heat from the room causes some of the food to thaw and change from solid ice to a liquid form. The liquid is heated by the microwave and warms the frozen food next to it. This gradual process continues until the frozen food is defrosted. Usually, the outer edges of the food are overheated in this process and cook before the inner parts of the food thaw.

# No Hands!

*If someone asked you to pick up an ice cube, it would be easy.
You could use your fingers to grasp the ice cube and pick it up.
But suppose you were asked to pick it up without using your
fingers? Try this trick to learn how.*

## MATERIALS

2 ice cubes

paper towel

piece of string, 1 foot (30 cm) long

salt shaker

ice bucket (insulated)

helper

## THE SETUP

1. Make ice cubes in your freezer several days in advance. Right
   before the magic show, place the ice cubes in the ice bucket.

2. Place the paper towel on the table. Put the string, ice bucket, and
   salt shaker next to it.

## MAGIC SCIENCE TIME!

1. Pick a member of the audience to be your helper. Take one ice
   cube from the ice bucket and place it on the paper towel. Ask your
   helper to pick up the ice cube. He should be able to do this without
   too much trouble.

2. Next ask your helper to pick up the ice cube without touching it.
   Say "You can use the string if you think it will help." After your
   helper decides the ice cube cannot be lifted without touching it, it's
   your turn to show how it can be done.

3. Take the other ice cube from the ice bucket and place it on the
   paper towel.

4. Place the string on top of the ice cube.

**5.** Sprinkle salt on the ice cube.

**6.** Wait about 1 minute, then lift the string.

## MAGIC SCIENCE TRICK TIPS

It's a good technique to use people from the audience as helpers. They get to be closer to the action, and you will become more comfortable doing the tricks with someone standing close to you.

Often, as in this trick, the helper gets a chance to try the trick before you. The helper cannot perform the trick, so when you do it, the audience is even more amazed.

## EFFECT

When your helper tries to lift the ice cube without using his or her hands, it cannot be done. When you lift the string, however, the ice cube is stuck to it.

## EXPLANATION

Liquid water freezes and turns into ice at a temperature of 32°F (0°C). But if you add another substance to the water, the temperature must be lower in order for the water to freeze. Water is a polar molecule (one end has a positive charge and the other end has the opposite, negative, charge). When water freezes, the water molecules move closer as the positive end of one water molecule attracts the negative end of another water molecule. If salt is added to the ice, the salt molecules, which also contain positive and negative particles, are also attracted to oppositely charged water molecules in the ice and the ice begins to melt. When you put salt on the ice cube, some of the ice melts and forms water, but the rest of the ice cube remains frozen. When you add the string and wait a minute, the water refreezes around the string. When you lift the string, the ice cube is attached to it.

In areas where it gets snowy and icy in the winter, salt is placed on roads. The salt lowers the temperature at which water turns to ice. When snow falls on the road, it remains water rather than turning to ice.

# PROJECT 3 Obedient Diver

*A good magician can make objects obey commands without touching them. Build this device to make an eye dropper obey your command.*

## MATERIALS

eyedropper

plastic drinking glass

tap water

½-gallon (2-liter) plastic soda bottle with screw-on lid (empty and clean)

## THE SETUP

1. Put the eyedropper into a glass of water to make sure that it floats. Squeeze the bulb end and draw in a small amount of water. If the eyedropper still floats, add more water. If it sinks, squeeze out some of the water. Keep drawing in or squeezing out water until you get the dropper to just barely float upright in the water.

2. Fill the bottle to the very top with water. Make sure there are no air bubbles trapped inside the bottle.

3. Transfer the dropper to the bottle. Screw the lid tightly on the bottle.

## MAGIC SCIENCE TIME!

1. Tell the audience, "With my magical powers I can make the eyedropper in the bottle obey my command without touching it."

2. Say some magic words, then gently squeeze the bottle. What happens? Say a few more magic words, then relax your grip on the bottle. What happens?

When you squeeze the bottle, the dropper falls. When you relax your grip, it rises again.

## E X P L A N A T I O N

Water is made of molecules that are continually sliding past one another and moving around. This movement creates a pressure called **water pressure**. When you squeeze the bottle, the water molecules are compressed, or pushed closer together. The water pressure inside the bottle, including the water pressure inside the eyedropper, increases as you squeeze and pushes against the air inside the eyedropper. You can actually see the level of water inside the dropper rise. As the water level inside the dropper rises, it squeezes the air in the dropper into a smaller space. This increased water pressure makes the dropper plus the water inside it more dense than the water around it, and the eyedropper sinks.

When you relax your grip, the water pressure in the bottle decreases. The air inside the eyedropper returns to its former level. The dropper becomes lighter than the surrounding water and starts to rise. This device is called a **Cartesian diver**, named after Rene Descartes, a sixteenth-century French mathematician.

**PROJECT**

# 4 Floating Paper Clip

*A magician seems to do things that are impossible. But can a magician make a metal object float? Check out this trick to learn how.*

## M A T E R I A L S

drinking glass
tap water
2 paper clips
paper towel

## THE SETUP

1. Fill the glass with water.

2. Unfold one of the paper clips to create a hook with a flat surface as shown.

## MAGIC SCIENCE TIME!

1. Tell the audience, "Everyone knows that paper clips don't float." To prove your point drop a paper clip in the glass of water.

2. Take the paper clip out of the glass and dry it off. Next, tell the audience that you are going to make this paper clip float.

3. Say a few magic words to the paper clip. Place the paper clip on the flat surface of the unfolded paper-clip hook. Hold it horizontally above the water, as close as possible to the surface of the water but without touching it.

4. Slowly lower the paper clip into the water.

## MAGIC SCIENCE TRICK TIPS

If the paper clip doesn't float on the surface of the water, try rubbing it against a candle before lowering it into the water.

## MORE FUN STUFF TO DO

Try floating other metal objects on the surface of the water. Can you float a sewing needle on the water?

## EFFECT

The paper clip floats on the water.

## EXPLANATION

The paper clip floats on the surface of the water because of a special property of water called **surface tension**. Water molecules are polar molecules. The positive part of one molecule is attracted to the negative part of another. Each water molecule is attracted in all directions to the water molecules that surround it.

However, the water molecules on the surface of water have no molecules above them, so they are only attracted to those next to and underneath them. This attraction creates a tension like a thin skin on the surface of the water. The surface tension of water is strong enough to support the paper clip.

It is important to lay the paper clip flat and lower it gently if you want it to float. If the clip strikes the surface at an angle, or hits the surface with a great force, the surface tension is broken and the water will not be able to float the paper clip.

## PROJECT

# 5 Scared Pepper

*Try this activity to make pepper move without touching it.*

## MATERIALS

1 cup (250 ml) cold tap water
shallow baking pan
ruler
pepper shaker
bar of soap

## THE SETUP

1. Pour the water into the baking pan. The water should be about ½-inch (1.25 cm) deep.

2. Let the pan rest until the water is no longer moving.

# Magic Science Time!

1. Tell the audience, "It's time for my pepper to take a bath. (Proper pepper should take a bath at least once a week.) The problem is that my pepper is afraid of soap. Let me show you what I mean."

2. Sprinkle pepper on the surface of the water. Use enough pepper to cover the entire surface of the water.

3. Touch the bar of soap to the center of the water. Watch what happens.

## MORE FUN STUFF TO DO

Try this activity with a loop of string in place of the pepper. Tie the ends of a piece of string in a knot to form a loop. Float the string in the center of the surface of the water. Touch the soap to the water inside the loop of string. Watch what happens.

## EFFECT

When you touch the bar of soap to the center of the water the pepper moves to the outside of the pan.

## EXPLANATION

Soap can break the surface tension of the water. When you touch soap to the water, some of it dissolves and mixes with the water. The soap molecules get between the water molecules and decrease the attraction they have for one another. The soap breaks the surface tension of the water in the area where you touch it. The tension on the rest of the surface of the water pulls the floating pepper to the sides of the pan, away from the soap.

In the More Fun Stuff to Do activity, the string moves outward and forms a circle. This happens because the soap breaks the surface tension of the water inside the loop. The string is then pulled outward by the force of the surface tension outside the circle.

# PROJECT 6 Air-Tight Cloth

*It's easy to understand how a jar can hold water. But can a piece of cloth? Find out in this activity.*

## MATERIALS

square piece of cheesecloth, 6-by-6 inches (15-by-15 cm)
drinking glass
rubber band
pitcher of tap water
plastic tub or baking pan

## THE SETUP

Place all of the materials on the table in front of you.

# MAGIC SCIENCE TIME!

1. Tell the audience, "I have a magic one-way cloth that only lets water go through it in one direction."

2. Place the cheesecloth over the mouth of the glass.

3. Wrap the rubber band around the cloth and the glass to hold the cloth in place. Hold the edges of the cloth against the side of the glass.

4. Pour tap water through the cloth to fill the glass to the top.

5. Hold the glass and edges of cloth with one hand and put your other hand over the mouth of the glass.

6. Turn the glass upside down over the plastic tub or baking pan.

7. Say a few magic words, then slowly remove your hand from the mouth of the glass. What happens?

glass

cheesecloth

rubber band

This trick works best if the glass is filled with water to the very top. If you have trouble getting the water to remain in the glass, soak the cheesecloth in water before you place it on the mouth of the glass.

## MORE FUN STUFF TO DO

Try other kinds of cloth to see if they work just as well.

### EFFECT

When you turn the glass over, a small amount of water leaks out, but eventually stops. The cloth stops water from flowing out of the glass.

### EXPLANATION

This trick works in part because of surface tension, which is the tendency of molecules to cling together at the surface of a liquid to form a skinlike film. The holes in the cloth fill with water and become sealed because of the surface tension of the water.

In addition, air, like water, contains molecules. These air molecules are always moving, creating a constant pressure called **air pressure**. When you turn the glass over, no air is left in the glass, thus there is no air pressure inside the glass. The pressure of the air outside the glass against the cloth is greater than the pressure of the water inside the glass against the cloth. The pressure of the water inside the glass against the cloth is caused by the force of Earth's **gravity** on the water. Gravity is the force of attraction between two objects due to their mass. The combination of air pressure against the cloth and the surface tension of the water allows the cloth to hold back the water.

# 7  Hot Hands

*We have all seen water boil. But can the heat from your finger boil water? Try this activity to find out.*

## MATERIALS

square piece of cheesecloth, 6-by-6 inches (15-by-15 cm)

drinking glass

rubber band

pitcher of tap water

plastic tub or baking pan

helper

## THE SETUP

1. Place the cheesecloth on top of the glass. Secure the cloth in place with the rubber band as shown.

2. Push the cheesecloth down slightly into the mouth of the glass so that it is not stretched tightly.

## MAGIC SCIENCE TIME!

1. Tell the audience, "In my last trick, I showed you how cheesecloth can stop water from flowing out of a glass. Now I am going to use the heat from one of your fingers to make the water boil."

2. Ask someone from the audience to be your helper.

3. Pour tap water through the cheesecloth into the glass until the glass is totally full.

4. Hold the glass and edges of cloth with one hand and put your other hand over the mouth of the glass.

5. Turn the glass upside down over the tub and remove your hand from the mouth of the glass.

6. Have your helper place a finger near the cheesecloth under the glass. Nothing will happen at first. Tell your helper, "Your finger is not hot enough. Rub it on the palm of your other hand to make it hotter."

**7.** After your helper rubs finger on palm, again have him or her place the finger near the cheesecloth under the glass.

**8.** Place your free hand on the bottom of the glass, and slowly push on the bottom of the glass as you pull the cheesecloth with the hand that is holding the glass.

## MAGIC SCIENCE TRICK TIPS

Do this trick right after "Air-Tight Cloth."

## EFFECT

When your helper places a warm finger under the cheesecloth, and you push on the bottom of the glass while pulling the cheesecloth, bubbles begin to move up through the water.

## EXPLANATION

As you learned in "Air-Tight Cloth," surface tension and air pressure keep the water in the glass, even after the glass has been turned upside down.

You did not fill the glass completely in this trick. When you push the cheesecloth down slightly in the mouth of the glass so that it is not stretched tightly, the volume of water in the glass is less. When you push on the bottom of the glass while pulling the cheesecloth, you increase the volume of the glass slightly. The increase in volume lowers the air pressure inside the glass compared to the air pressure outside the glass. Air from the outside is forced through the cloth, in spite of the surface tension, and is seen as air bubbles rising in the glass.

# PROJECT

## 8 Twister!

*You may have seen a movie about tornadoes. But did you know that you can make one? Try this activity to learn how.*

### MATERIALS

2 ½-gallon (2-liter) plastic soda bottles (empty and clean)

tap water

1-inch (2.5-cm) metal washer

duct tape

### THE SETUP

1. Fill one of the bottles two-thirds full of water.

2. Place the metal washer over the opening of the bottle.

3. Turn the second bottle upside down and place it on the washer.

4. Use the duct tape to fasten the two containers and the metal washer together. Use several layers of tape to make sure that there will be no water leaks when you turn the bottles over.

### MAGIC SCIENCE TIME!

1. Tell your audience that you are going to make a tornado.

2. Turn the bottles over so that the bottle with the water is on top.

3. Place the bottles on the table. A small amount of water will begin to trickle from the top bottle to the bottom bottle. Tell the audience, "I forgot one important thing—wind. All tornadoes need some wind to get them started."

4. Make a wind sound. Hold the bottles tightly and move them quickly in a small circle horizontally. Watch what happens.

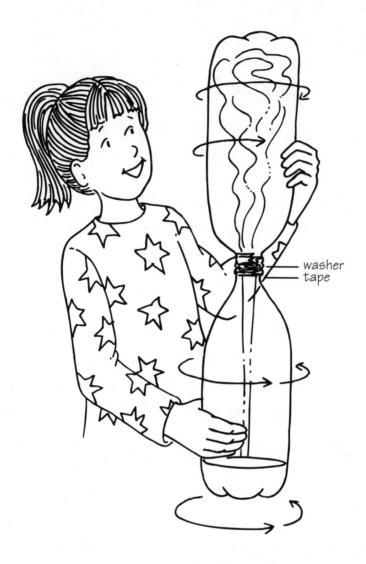

washer
tape

## Magic Science Trick Tips

Another way to introduce a trick is to involve your audience in the trick you are about to do. Before you begin this trick, ask if anyone in the audience has ever seen a tornado, either in a movie or in real life. If someone says yes, have the person tell other members of the audience about the tornado. He or she will probably talk about the swirling winds that make up the tornado. You can use this description to talk about the tornado you make in this trick.

## Effect

The water will spin in a circle as it moves from the top bottle to the bottom bottle.

## EXPLANATION

There are two forces at work in this activity. (A **force** is something that changes the shape or movement of an object.) One force is gravity, the force of attraction between all objects. Gravity pulls all objects to Earth, including water. Gravity pulls the water in the top bottle toward the bottom bottle. But gravity alone is not enough to create the tornado effect. The air in the bottom bottle also exerts a force. When you first turn the bottles over, the water in the top bottle begins to flow into the bottom bottle but then stops. The force of the air or air pressure in the bottom bottle stops the flow of the water.

When you swirl the bottles, a small tornado forms. In the center of the water tornado is a hole. The hole goes from the top of the water to the opening between the two bottles. The hole allows air from the bottom bottle to escape to the top bottle as the water moves. As the air escapes from the bottom bottle, the air pressure in the two bottles becomes equal. Gravity is then the only force acting on the water.

When the water is in the top bottle, it has potential energy. **Potential energy** is energy that is stored for later use. When you swirl the bottles, you give the water movement, or kinetic energy. **Kinetic energy** is energy that is being used. As the water swirls from the top bottle to the bottom bottle, it changes its potential energy into kinetic energy. The movement of the water from the top bottle to the bottom bottle helps to keep the water spinning in the tornado effect.

## PROJECT
# 9 Broken Pencil

*You've used water in the previous activities to perform some amazing tricks. In this activity you'll use water and light to perform an interesting illusion.*

## MATERIALS
glass
tap water
pencil

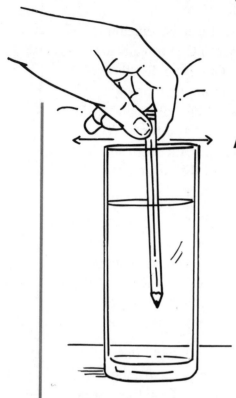

## THE SETUP

1. Fill the glass about two-thirds full of tap water.

2. Place the glass of water and pencil on the table.

## MAGIC SCIENCE TIME!

1. Hold the pencil in front of you. Tell the audience, "I am going to break the pencil by simply sticking it in this glass of water."

2. Hold the pencil upright in the water so that the tip is about halfway between the surface of the water and the bottom of the glass.

3. Hold the pencil near the back of the glass, away from the audience.

4. Move the pencil back and forth in the water, keeping it upright. Ask them what they see.

5. Remove the pencil from the water.

## EFFECT

The pencil looks broken to the audience. The part of the pencil that is not in the water seems to be in one place, while the part of the pencil in the water seems to be slightly off in one direction or another.

## EXPLANATION

This trick works because of **refraction**. Light travels in straight lines, but when it travels from one transparent substance to another the light rays bend. This is refraction. When light travels from a more dense transparent substance, such as water, to a less dense substance, such as air, the light refracts, or bends noticeably. Light travels at different speeds in substances with different densities.

Light reflected from the pencil appears to the audience to be in one place when it travels to their eyes through the air, and in another place when it is refracted through the water.

# 10 Disappearing Penny

*Here's another activity that uses light and water to produce a mind-boggling effect.*

## MATERIALS

1 quart (1 liter) glass jar with lid

tap water

penny

helper

## THE SETUP

1. Fill the jar with tap water. Put the lid on the jar.

2. Place the jar and penny on the table in front of you.

## MAGIC SCIENCE TIME!

1. Ask a member of the audience to be your helper.

2. Ask your helper to take the penny and make sure that it is definitely a penny, and to check that there is nothing wrong with the penny.

3. Have your helper place the penny on the table. Ask "Can you see it?" (Helper will answer yes.)

4. Place the jar filled with water on top of the penny.

5. Say a few magic words, such as "Magic penny, here today. Magic penny, go away."

6. Ask your helper to look through the water from the side of the jar and see if the penny is there or gone. What is the answer?

## MAGIC SCIENCE TRICK TIPS

You can make this trick even better. After your helper cannot see the penny, you then make it reappear. Say some more magic words, like "Magic penny, gone away. Magic penny, come back to stay." Then take the jar off the penny, and there it is.

## EFFECT

When you put the jar filled with water over the penny, the penny will seem to disappear. Your helper will not see it.

## EXPLANATION

When light travels from a less dense substance, such as air, to a more dense substance, such as water, the light refracts, or changes directions, at the boundary between the two substances. Traveling from air to water, light bends toward the **normal**, a line perpendicular to the surface. Traveling from water to air, light bends in the opposite direction, away from the normal.

This trick works because at a certain angle, when light travels from a more dense substance (water), to a less dense substance (air), it no longer refracts but will reflect. **Reflection** is the bouncing back of light from a surface. When the image of the penny comes toward the side surface of the jar at too great an angle, reflection rather than refraction occurs, and the image cannot be seen outside of the jar.

light from penny

penny under jar

# The Magic of Air

## Working Under Pressure

The air that surrounds us is a gas. Gases and liquids are considered fluids. **Fluids** are substances that flow and can change their shape easily. Air contains molecules that move around freely, allowing air to change shape to fit a certain space. This movement of air molecules creates a constant pressure called air pressure.

We can't see the air, but we know it's there because of what it does. We feel the wind on our bodies and see it blowing through the trees.

To learn more about how magicians use air and air pressure to perform some of their magic tricks, try the activities in this chapter.

# PROJECT

# Keeping Dry

*Air can be used in many magic tricks. Try this activity to learn one way air can amaze your audience.*

## MATERIALS

paper towel

drinking glass

plastic tub or bucket filled with enough tap water to reach the height of the glass

## THE SETUP

Place the materials on the table.

## MAGIC SCIENCE TIME!

1. Tell the audience, "I have special powers that can keep a piece of paper dry."

2. Crumple the paper towel and place it in the bottom of the glass.

3. Turn the glass over and make sure that the paper will stay in place at the bottom of the glass.

4. Say a few magic words over the glass, such as "Magic force, protect the paper from the water." Then slowly lower the upside-

down glass into the tub of water. Keep the glass as straight up and down as possible, until the entire glass is under water.

5. Take the glass out of the water and let the water drip off the glass.

6. Turn the glass right side up and remove the paper towel. Let audience members feel the paper towel to determine if it is wet or dry.

## EFFECT

The audience discovers that the paper towel is dry.

## EXPLANATION

Air takes up space. The glass is filled with air when it is right side up and when it is upside down. When you turn the glass over and slowly lower it into the water, air remains in the glass. The water cannot enter the glass because of the air inside the glass. The air creates pressure that is greater than the pressure of the water trying to get in. The towel in the top of the glass stays dry. If you were to tilt the glass on its side in the water, air would exit the glass in the form of bubbles. Water would then be able to enter the glass.

## PROJECT 2 Fat Air

*The air we breathe keeps us alive. If that isn't magic enough, try this activity to see how air can help you perform more magic.*

## MATERIALS

safety glasses or goggles

¼-by-1-by-24 inches (.3-by-2.5-by-60 cm) pine stick (this can be purchased at any lumber store)

sheet of newspaper

ruler

## The Setup

Put the materials on the table.

## Magic Science Time!

1.  Put on your safety glasses or goggles. Tell the audience, "There are two kinds of air in the world. Some air is skinny and some air is fat. I am going to use the fat air to help me perform a magic trick."

2.  Place the stick on the table so that about 6 inches (15 cm) extends over the edge of the table.

3.  Say, "Fat air, sit on the stick." Hit the part of the stick that extends over the table's edge. The stick will flip up into the air.

4.  Tell the audience that skinny air must have sat on the stick. Place the stick back over the table's edge as you did in Step 2.

5.  Lay the sheet of newspaper over the stick as shown, with the stick centered under the newspaper. Flatten out the newspaper so there is no air between it and the table.

6.  Again say, "Fat air, sit on the stick." Using the edge of your palm hit the protruding end of the stick.

## EFFECT

When you first hit the stick, it flips. But when you hit the stick with the newspaper on it, the stick breaks.

## EXPLANATION

When you flatten out the newspaper, you push almost all the air out from under it. However, a large amount of air above the newspaper pushes down on the paper with great pressure. When you hit the stick, the stick breaks because the force of the air pressure above the newspaper keeps the stick from moving up in response to your force.

## PROJECT 3  Do Not Disturb

*Is air pressure strong enough to keep water in a glass when you turn it upside down? Try this activity to find out.*

## MATERIALS

scissors
thin cardboard
ruler
drinking glass
felt-tip marker
plastic dishpan or glass baking pan
pitcher of tap water

## THE SETUP

1. Use the scissors to cut a square piece of cardboard so that it is about 1 inch (2.5 cm) larger than the mouth of the glass on all sides.

2. Use the marker to write "Do Not Disturb" on the cardboard.

3. Place the dishpan, glass, pitcher of water, and piece of cardboard on your table.

# MAGIC SCIENCE TIME!

1. Tell the audience that you are going to use a thin piece of cardboard to keep water in an upside down glass.

2. Fill the glass with water until it is completely full.

3. Place the cardboard over the mouth of the glass so that the writing is on top.

4. Place one hand on top of the cardboard and turn the glass upside down over the dishpan while holding the cardboard in place.

5. Say a few magic words, then slowly remove the hand holding the cardboard in place.

# MAGIC SCIENCE TRICK TIPS

Your hand holding the card must be dry so that when you remove the hand, it won't stick to the cardboard.

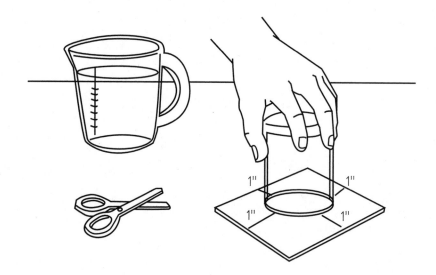

Try the activity with different amounts of water in the glass or with different kinds of cardboard or other materials holding the water in the glass. Will it work with the glass half or three-quarters full of water or with a square of thin plastic instead of cardboard?

## EFFECT

When you remove your hand from the card, the water stays in the glass and does not pour out.

## EXPLANATION

This trick works because of surface tension, which is the tendency of molecules to cling together at the surface of a liquid to form a skin-like film. The surface tension of the water seals the area between the cardboard and the glass. This keeps the cardboard stuck to the glass, but that's not the only thing keeping the water in the glass.

The upside down glass holds the water because the air pressure outside the glass pushes against the cardboard. The air pressure against the cardboard is greater than the water pressure on the inside of the glass and the water cannot pour out. The water pressure inside of the glass is caused by the gravity trying to pull the water toward the Earth.

If you tried the More Fun Stuff to Do, you found out that the trick still works even when the glass is half full. The force of air outside the glass against the cardboard is greater that the water pressure on the inside of the glass and the water cannot pour out.

# 4 Sticking Cup

*Try this activity to learn how to use air pressure to stick objects to one another.*

## MATERIALS

2 large balloons
2 1-cup (250-ml) plastic cups
helper

## THE SETUP

Place the materials on the table before you start the trick.

## MAGIC SCIENCE TIME!

1. Pick someone from the audience to be your helper.

2. Give your helper a balloon and a cup, and keep a balloon and cup for yourself.

3. Ask your helper to blow up his or her balloon about half way, then twist the end and hold it closed so that the air cannot escape.

4. Next ask your helper to try to stick the cup to the balloon. When he or she cannot do it, it's your turn.

5. Blow up your balloon about one-third full of air. Hold your cup against the side of the balloon.

6. With the cup in place, continue to blow up the balloon until the balloon is at least two-thirds full of air. Release the cup.

## MAGIC SCIENCE TRICK TIPS

Show the audience that the cup is not glued to the balloon by letting air out of the balloon. The cup will fall off.

Try sticking two cups to the balloon at the same time. This will take some practice and a hand from a helper. Have your helper hold two cups to the balloon, then blow up the balloon as you previously did.

## EFFECT

When you blow up the balloon, the cup sticks to the side.

## EXPLANATION

As you hold the cup to the balloon and blow it up, the balloon flattens across the mouth of the cup. When the balloon flattens, the volume of air in the cup increases slightly, meaning there is slightly more space available in the cup. However, the number of air molecules in the cup doesn't change, so there is less air pressure in the cup. The air pressure in the cup is less than the air pressure outside. The difference in air pressure inside and outside the cup holds the cup in place.

# PROJECT 5

# Refusing Funnel

*Can a funnel "refuse" to let water into a bottle? Check it out in this activity.*

## MATERIALS

2 funnels

two identical 1-quart (1-liter) plastic bottles (clean and dry)

plasticine clay

pitcher of tap water

## THE SETUP

1. Put a funnel in the opening of each bottle.

2. Use the plasticine clay to fill in the area around the funnel on one of the bottles to seal the opening.

## MAGIC SCIENCE TIME!

1. Tell the audience, "I have a magic funnel that refuses to let water into a bottle."

2. Take the bottle without the clay and pour some of the tap water into the funnel. Tell the audience, "This is the way most funnels should act."

3. Place the bottle with the clay on the table.

4. Fill the funnel to the top with water. Watch what happens.

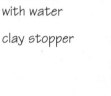

funnel filled with water

clay stopper

## EFFECT

A few drops of water from the funnel will drip into the bottle then the flow of water will stop.

## EXPLANATION

This is another example of the power of air pressure. The first bottle allows water to go into it. When water is poured into it through the funnel, the water replaces the air in the bottle and the air leaves the bottle through the opening at the top. The sealed bottle with the funnel is filled with air, which has air pressure. The water in the funnel has a pressure as well, caused by the force of gravity pulling it down. However, the force of the air pressure in the bottle is greater than the force of gravity on the water. The water cannot enter the bottle.

If there is a small hole in the bottle or in the clay seal, then the air inside the bottle can escape. This decreases the air pressure inside the bottle, and the water can enter the bottle.

# PROJECT 6 Crusher!

*As you found in the previous activities, magicians can use air pressure to perform extraordinary magic tricks. Try this activity to see how air pressure can crush a can.*

**Note: This activity requires a stove or hot plate and adult help.**

## MATERIALS

pie pan

tap water

ruler

stove or hot plate (to be used only by adult helper)

empty soda can

tongs

adult helper

## THE SETUP

1. Fill the pie pan with about 1 inch (2.5 cm) of water. Place the pie pan on the counter next to the stove.

2. Place a small amount of water in the empty soda can—just enough to cover the bottom of the can.

3. Have an adult heat the soda can with water on a stove burner or hot plate. Let the water boil vigorously for about 1 minute. Steam should come out of the can.

## MAGIC SCIENCE TIME!

1. Tell the audience that you are going to crush the soda can without touching it.

2. Have your adult helper use the tongs to quickly turn the can upside down in the pie pan of water. Watch what happens!

## MAGIC SCIENCE TRICK TIPS

Before your helper turns the can upside down in the pie pan of water, say a few magic words. Move your hands above the can and say, "Soda can, I command you to collapse when water touches you!"

## MORE FUN STUFF TO DO

Try repeating this magic trick using a 1-quart (1-liter) can, such as a tomato juice can. When you open the can make only small holes in the top. Empty and clean out the can before using it, but do not remove the entire top of the can. Does this type of can collapse as easily as the soda can does?

## EFFECT

When your helper puts the can upside down in the pie pan filled with water, the can is immediately crushed.

## EXPLANATION

The can is crushed because of a change in air pressure. You create low air pressure inside the can, then you use the higher pressure outside the can to crush it.

Before you heat it, the can is filled with water and air. When you boil the water, it evaporates—it changes from liquid to hot water vapor or steam. The steam inside the can pushes the air out of the can. When your helper turns the can upside down in the water, air cannot go back inside the can.

The cool water in the pie pan cools the steam remaining in the can. The steam condenses—changes from gas to liquid water. The steam that took up the space inside the can now becomes a few drops of water, which take up much less space than the steam did. There is more room for the air in the can, so the air pressure inside the can drops. The pressure of the air outside of the can is then greater than the pressure inside the can. The air pushes on the can, causing the can to collapse.

## PROJECT 7 Air Ball

*Have you ever seen a magician make a person float in mid-air? Try this activity to learn your own version of that trick.*

**Note: This activity requires a blow-dryer and adult help.**

## MATERIALS

blow-dryer (to be used only by adult helper)

2 large books or other heavy objects

Ping-Pong ball

ruler

adult helper

## THE SETUP

1. Place the blow-dryer on the table with the exhaust end (the end the hot air comes out of) pointing up.

2. Use the books to hold the blow-dryer in place. Make sure that the books do not block the air intake fan on the side of the dryer.

3. Plug in the dryer.

## MAGIC SCIENCE TIME!

1. Ask an adult in the audience to be your helper.

2. Tell the audience, "I am going to make an ordinary Ping-Pong ball float in the air."

3. Hold the Ping-Pong ball in your hand and let it drop to the table. Tell the audience, "Whoops! I forgot to say the magic words!"

4. Say a few magic words over the Ping-Pong ball. Have your helper set the dryer to its highest setting and turn it on.

5. Carefully place the ball in the stream of air about 18 inches (45 cm) from the exhaust end of the dryer.

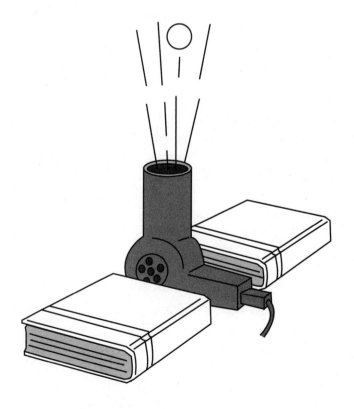

## MAGIC SCIENCE TRICK TIPS

It might be necessary to place the Ping-Pong ball slightly farther away from or closer to the exhaust end of the dryer depending on the force of the air.

## MORE FUN STUFF TO DO

Try this trick with balls of different sizes and weights. Do they all work equally well?

## EFFECT

The ball will stay suspended in mid-air above the blow-dryer.

## EXPLANATION

This trick doesn't actually defy gravity. It demonstrates an important property of air called Bernoulli's principle. **Bernoulli's principle** is a natural law that states that when any fluid, such as air, flows, its pressure decreases as its speed increases. In other words, when air flows very fast, its pressure is low. When the speed of the air flow is slow, its pressure is high.

The air coming out of the blow-dryer moves very fast and thus has a low pressure. An area of low pressure surrounds all sides of the ball, creating a cone of low pressure near the mouth of the blow-dryer. The air outside the cone has a higher pressure, which keeps the ball in the low-pressure cone. Gravity pulls the ball down as the force of the air pushes the ball up. These forces work together to keep the ball suspended in mid-air above the dryer.

# Stubborn Card

*If you blow on an index card, it will move away from you, right? Not always! Check it out in this activity.*

## MATERIALS

pencil
ruler
3-by-5-inch (7.5-by-12.5-cm) index card
thumbtack
empty thread spool
helper

## THE SETUP

1. Use the pencil and ruler to draw diagonal lines joining opposite corners on the index card. The point where the lines meet is the center of the card.

2. Push the thumbtack through the center of the card.

## MAGIC SCIENCE TIME!

1. Invite a member of the audience to be your helper.

2. Place the index card under the thread spool so that the thumbtack is in the hole of the thread spool.

3. Lift the card and the spool. Have your helper hold onto the spool and blow hard into the hole.

4. Take your hand away while your helper is still blowing.

5. Can your helper blow the card away?

## EFFECT

The card sticks to the thread spool and does not fall off.

## EXPLANATION

This trick also demonstrates Bernoulli's principle, which states that fast-moving air has lower pressure than slow-moving air. When your helper blows into the hole in the spool, a stream of fast-moving air is created on the spool side of the card. This fast-moving air creates an area of lower pressure between the spool and the card. The air pressure on the other side of the card is greater. It pushes the card against the spool, holding the card in place. When your helper stops blowing, the air pressure on both sides of the card is equal and the card falls off the spool.

# PROJECT 9  Attracting Cans

*In the previous activities, you've seen several ways that Bernoulli's principle can be used to perform magic tricks. Here's another way.*

## MATERIALS

2 empty soda cans
24 plastic drinking straws
helper

## THE SETUP

1. Place the two cans on the table about 1 inch (2.5 cm) apart.

2. Put the straws on the table near the cans.

## MAGIC SCIENCE TIME!

1. Ask a member of the audience to be your helper.

2. Ask your helper to make the cans move closer together by blowing air through one of the straws. Your helper might be able to make one can move a little closer to the other, but will find it difficult.

3. When it is your turn, set one straw aside. Spread the remaining 23 straws on the table parallel to one another and about ¼ to ½ inch (.625 to 1.25 cm) apart.

4. Stand the two cans on the straws about 3 inches (7.5 cm) apart. Tell the audience that you want an even bigger challenge, so you are placing the cans farther apart.

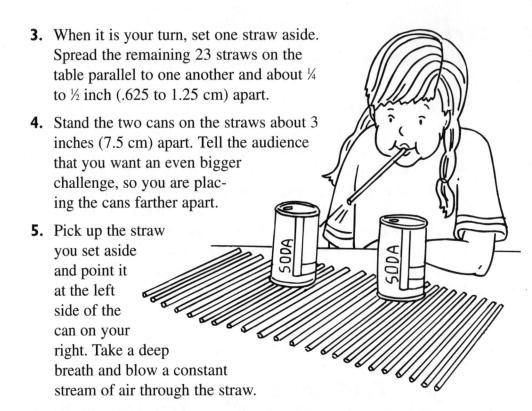

5. Pick up the straw you set aside and point it at the left side of the can on your right. Take a deep breath and blow a constant stream of air through the straw.

6. Keep blowing, moving your head and the straw to the left as the can moves.

## MAGIC SCIENCE TRICK TIPS

This trick works best if the straws are perfectly round.

## MORE FUN STUFF TO DO

Try this trick another way. Hang two empty soda cans from strings so that the cans are about 1 inch (2.5 cm) apart. Experiment with different ways to make the cans move together using the air blown through a straw. Will this trick work if you hang two apples the same distance apart?

## EFFECT

When you blow on the left side of one can, it moves toward the other can. In the More Fun Stuff To Do section, the cans and apples move toward each other when you blow in between them.

## EXPLANATION

Both of these activities again demonstrate Bernoulli's principle. When your helper tries to move the cans by blowing directly on them, he or she is not successful. However, you are able to make the cans move by blowing on one side of the can. When you blow on the side of the can you create fast-moving air on that side. Bernoulli's principle states that fast-moving air has lower pressure than slow-moving air, so your blowing creates an area of low pressure on the right side of the can. The higher pressure pushing on the left side of the can causes the can to move. The faster you blow, the lower the pressure, and the more the can will move. The straws under the cans reduce the friction between the cans and the table so the can moves more easily.

# PROJECT 10 Magic Motor

*Try this activity to see how you can use air to make paper magically move like a motor.*

## MATERIALS

glue
1-by-1-inch (2.5-by-2.5 cm) square piece of wood or a wooden block
sewing needle
3-by-3-inch (7.5-by 7.5 cm) square piece of paper

## THE SETUP

1. Place a drop of glue in the center of the piece of wood.

2. Hold the eye end of the needle in the glue at a right angle (perpendicular) to the wood. Hold it steady until the glue dries enough so that the needle can stand by itself. Set the wood and needle assembly aside until it dries completely.

**3.** Fold the paper in half diagonally (from corner to corner). Open the paper and fold it again diagonally using the opposite corners. Open the paper again. The place where the folds meet is the center of the paper. The paper will look like a low, partially flattened pyramid.

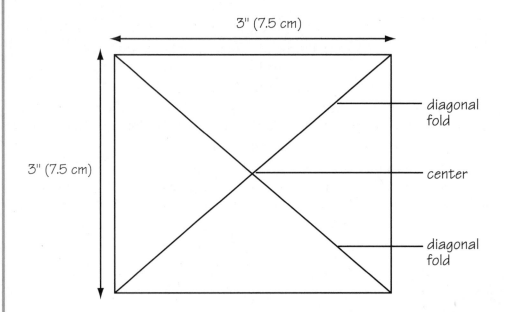

## MAGIC SCIENCE TIME!

**1.** Tell the audience, "I have found a magical power that can run a small paper motor."

**2.** Place the wood and needle assembly on the table.

**3.** Place the folded paper on the point of the needle by placing the center of the two folds on the point of the needle. The four sides of the pyramid should point down.

**4.** Say a few magic words, such as, "Magic energy, make my motor turn."

**5.** Rub your hands together about 5 to 10 times, then cup them around the paper pyramid. Your hands should be about 1 inch (2.5 cm) from the edges of the paper. Watch what happens.

## EFFECT

The paper wobbles at first, then starts to rotate in a circle.

## EXPLANATION

Believe it or not, it's the heat from your hands that causes the paper to move. When you rub your hands together, you create friction, the force that slows down the movement of objects over each other. Friction makes things hot, so the friction between your hands produces heat.

Heat always moves from something warmer to something cooler. Air that comes in contact with your warm hands gets warmer. The warmer air rises because it expands and becomes less dense, so it is lighter. Cooler, dense air falls down to take its place. As the air moves, it comes in contact with the paper pyramid, causing it to move as well.

This movement of warmer and cooler air is called **convection**. Convection is the process by which heat travels in moving currents through fluids (liquids and gases).

# The Magic of Force and Energy

## "Force-Full" Feats

Energy—the ability to do work—is a very important part of life. Nothing would happen without energy. And whenever energy is used, some kind of force or forces must be present. Forces change the shape of things or make them stop or start moving. Gravity is the force of attraction between any two objects due to their mass. We take gravity for granted. It holds us onto Earth and keeps us from flying into space. Gravity is the magic that holds our universe together.

You can use gravity and other forces to perform all sorts of magic tricks. Try the activities in this chapter to learn all about it.

## PROJECT

# Catch It!

*A magician often asks a member of the audience to do something that seems easy, but turns out to be impossible. Try this activity to learn one way to do this.*

### MATERIALS

dollar bill
helper

### THE SETUP

Place the dollar bill on the table in front of you.

### MAGIC SCIENCE TIME!

1. Hold up the dollar bill and let it fall to the table.

2. Ask someone in the audience to be your helper. Tell the audience that you will let the helper have the dollar bill if he or she can catch it after you drop it.

3. Fold the bill in half lengthwise.

4. Tell your helper, "Make a fist and hold it out in front of you." Next, have helper open thumb and index finger so that there is a space between the thumb and index finger.

**5.** Hold the bill upright between your helper's finger and thumb so about half of the bill extends below the finger and thumb. Tell your helper that you are going to let go of the bill. He or she should try to catch the bill after you drop it by pinching finger and thumb together.

**6.** Release the bill.

## MAGIC SCIENCE TRICK TIPS

Talk to your helper before you release the dollar bill. Keep talking and then release the dollar bill in the middle of a sentence. The talking will distract your helper so he or she won't know exactly when you are going to release the dollar bill.

## EFFECT

The helper is not able to catch the dollar bill before it falls past his or her finger and thumb.

Gravity pulls all objects to Earth at the same rate no matter how much they weigh. A dollar bill is about 6 inches (15 cm) long. When the middle of the dollar is placed between your helper's fingers, it only has to fall 3 inches (7.5 cm) before it falls past your helper's fingers. It will take less than .2 seconds for the dollar bill to fall that distance. It takes about .3 seconds for your helper's brain to send his or her fingers the message to close. There is not enough time for your helper to react before the dollar bill falls out of reach.

It is possible to catch the bill. Your helper must correctly predict when you are going to release the bill and then begin to close the fingers ahead of time.

## PROJECT 2

# Find the Middle

*It is easy to find the middle of a piece of wood using a tape measure. But can you find it without one? Try this trick to see how.*

## M A T E R I A L S

wooden broomstick or dowel, about 2 to 3 feet (60 to 90 cm) long
yardstick, meterstick, or tape measure
helper

## T H E  S E T U P

Place the broomstick on the table.

## M A G I C  S C I E N C E  T I M E !

1. Tell the audience, "I have magical powers in my hands. I'm going to use my powers to find the middle of this piece of wood without using a tape measure."

2. Hold the broomstick at about waist height. Rest it on your index fingers. Your fingers should be about 2 feet (60 cm) apart.

**3.** Slowly move your fingers toward each other, keeping the broom-stick resting on them.

**4.** When your fingers meet and the broomstick is balanced, you have found the center of the broomstick.

**5.** Set the broomstick on the table, keeping one of your fingers on the center point. Invite a member of the audience to use the measuring stick or tape measure to verify that you've located the center.

Repeat the activity, but place a large lump of clay on one end of the broomstick. Can you still find the center of the broomstick?

## EFFECT

Your fingers will meet in the center of the broomstick.

## EXPLANATION

You are able to find the center of the broomstick because of gravity. The point at which the broomstick balances on your fingers (or at which any object balances) is called the **center of gravity**. The center of gravity of an object is where the effect of gravity on that object seems to be concentrated. For a symmetrical object, such as the broomstick, the center of gravity will also be the center of the object. A **symmetrical** object is one that is exactly the same on both sides of its center.

As you slide your fingers from the ends of the broomstick toward the center, small differences in friction cause one finger to stick to the broomstick. The other finger then continues moving toward the center of gravity. However, once that finger moves closer to the center of gravity, the force of gravity on that finger increases. This creates greater friction on that finger. The first finger, which had previously stopped, starts to move. This stopping and starting continues until both fingers meet at the center of gravity.

# PROJECT 3
## Raw or Cooked?

*A magician can often predict things that other people cannot. Try this activity to learn one way.*

***Note: This activity requires adult help.***

### MATERIALS

hard-cooked egg

raw egg

small bowl

adult helper

### THE SETUP

1. Have an adult hard cook an egg for you. Let the egg cool to room temperature.

2. Place the materials on the table.

### MAGIC SCIENCE TIME!

1. Tell the audience that you have two identical eggs, one raw and one hard cooked. Invite several members of the audience to come up and try to figure out which is which—without breaking the eggs!

2. When the audience members determine that they cannot tell the difference, you take over.

3. On the table, spin both eggs on their sides at the same time and with the same force. Point to the egg spinning faster and making more even spins and tell the audience that that is the hard-cooked egg.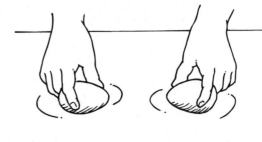

4. Crack the other egg into the bowl to prove that you have picked the right egg.

Have a second raw egg and a paper towel ready after you finish the trick. Ask several members of the audience to try to balance the second raw egg on its end on the paper towel. After they cannot do it, you can show them how it is done.

Hold the raw egg in your hand and shake it vigorously, lengthwise, up and down for about 30 seconds. Immediately place it on its larger end on the paper. It should stand up fine.

## EFFECT

The hard-cooked egg will spin faster and make more even spins than the raw egg. The raw egg will wobble when it spins.

## EXPLANATION

This trick works because the center of gravity of a raw egg is different from that of a cooked egg. A chicken egg consists of yoke, egg white, and shell. The yoke is where most of the mass is concentrated, so the center of gravity of the egg is close to the yoke, or in the yoke. When a raw egg is spun, the yoke moves around so the center of gravity keeps changing, slowing down the egg's spin and causing the egg to wobble. When the egg is hard cooked, the mass inside the egg is solid. The center of gravity is stationary and the egg can spin faster around this point.

The More Fun Stuff to Do activity works because when you shake the egg, the yoke moves around more easily inside the egg white. After you finish shaking the egg, the yoke moves to the wide end of the egg. This lowers the center of gravity of the egg, making it much more stable. Balancing works best if an object has a low center of gravity. Even if you shake it, it is almost impossible to balance an egg on its smaller end because the center of gravity is too high.

# PROJECT 4

# Broom and Ball

*You may have seen a magician pull a tablecloth from beneath a glass of water without losing a drop. Try this activity to find out how to do an even more spectacular trick.*

## MATERIALS

plastic drinking glass (**CAUTION: You must use a *plastic* drinking glass. *Do not* substitute one made of glass.**)

metal pie plate

empty toilet paper tube

golf ball

yardstick or meterstick

bristle broom

## THE SETUP

Put all the materials on the table before you start the trick.

## MAGIC SCIENCE TIME!

1. Tell the audience that you are going to do an amazing trick that other magicians won't even try.

2. Place the plastic glass near the edge of your table.

3. Place the pie plate right-side-up on top of the glass. The plate should stick out over the edge of the table.

4. Place the toilet paper tube upright on the pie plate so that it is directly above the glass.

5. Place the golf ball on the top of the toilet paper tube.

6. Hold the broom upright in front of you. Stand about 2 feet (60 cm) from the golf ball tower, facing the tower.

7. Bend the broom's bristles toward you, then step on them to hold them to the floor.

8. Ask the audience for quiet, saying something like, "I don't want to be disturbed in this, the most difficult trick of all time!"

9. Pull the broom toward you, then release it so that the broomstick hits the pie plate.

## MORE FUN STUFF TO DO

You'll need to practice this trick several times before trying it in front of an audience. Once you have mastered it, try using an egg at the top of the tower instead of the golf ball. Fill the plastic drinking glass with water to keep the egg from breaking.

## EFFECT

The broomstick hits the plate and pushes the plate and toilet paper tube out from under the golf ball. The golf ball falls into the plastic cup.

## EXPLANATION

This activity demonstrates **inertia**, which is the tendency of objects to resist a change in motion. The **law of inertia** states that an object at rest stays at rest, and an object in motion stays in motion, unless acted on by an outside force.

At first the golf ball is at rest, supported against the force of gravity by the pie plate and toilet paper tube. When you release the broom, it strikes the metal pie plate, creating an outside force on the plate. This force causes the pie plate to move. Some of this force is transferred to the toilet paper tube, and it moves as well.

The glass and the golf ball are not acted on by the outside force, however, so they remain at rest. As soon as the pie plate and toilet paper tube are out of the way, gravity pulls the ball downward into the glass.

# PROJECT
# 5 Impossible!

*Try this activity to learn how to use a force to overcome gravity.*

***Note: This activity requires adult help.***

## MATERIALS

metal coat hanger
file
penny
adult helper

## THE SETUP

I. Pull down the middle of the bottom of the coat hanger so that the hanger is long and narrow.

2. Stick your finger in the middle of the bend you created in Step 1, letting the hanger hang down freely.

3. Have an adult file the end of the hook on the opposite end of the hanger so that it is flat. Bend the hook so that when the hanger hangs from your finger, the flat end of the hook is level with the ground.

4. Place the materials on the table before starting the trick.

## MAGIC SCIENCE TIME!

1. Tell the audience that you have a special coat hanger that can defy gravity.

2. Place the bend of the hanger on the index finger of your hand.

3. Balance the penny on the flattened end of the wire hook as shown at right.

4. Start to swing the hanger, first slowly back and forth, then do full loops.

5. To stop swinging the hanger without the penny falling off, start swinging the hanger slower at the end of each swing. Return to swinging back and forth, slower and slower until you stop the action.

6. Remove the penny to show the audience that the penny was not glued to the end of the wire.

## MAGIC SCIENCE TRICK TIPS

This trick is difficult. You will need to practice many times before you are ready to perform this trick before an audience.

## EFFECT

The penny remains on the end of the wire even when you swing the hanger upside down.

All objects will remain at rest or keep moving in a straight line unless acted on by an outside force; this is the law of inertia. According to the law of inertia, the moving hanger causes the penny to move. The penny wants to move in a straight line but is acted on by an outside force, the hanger. The hanger causes the penny to move in a circle. Whenever you swing the penny or any object in a circle, the object is moving forward in a straight line, but a force pulls it inward toward the center of the circle. This force is **centripetal force**. Centripetal force changes the direction of the spinning penny so it goes in a circle and not in a straight line. If you let go of the hanger, you would remove the centripetal force and the penny would fly off in a straight line.

The force of gravity also comes into play in this activity. The force of gravity pulls the penny down, but the centripetal force created by the spinning motion is greater than the pull of gravity. The penny stays stuck to the end of the wire.

# PROJECT 6 Big Bounce

*If you have ever seen a Super Ball bounce, you know it can bounce very high. Try this trick to see how you can make a tennis ball bounce like a Super Ball.*

## MATERIALS

safety glasses or goggles

tennis ball

basketball

## THE SETUP

This trick is best done outside where there is a flat concrete sidewalk.

## MAGIC SCIENCE TIME!

1. Put on your safety glasses or goggles. Tell your audience, "I have a very special tennis ball. It can bounce higher than any Super Ball."

2. Hold the tennis ball at waist height and drop it. It will bounce like a normal ball.

3. Tell the audience that you forgot to say the magic words. Repeat a few magic words, such as "Magic ball bounce high, I command you."

4. Put one hand under the basketball and hold it at waist height. With the other hand, put the tennis ball on top of the basketball and hold it there.

5. Release both balls at the same time and let them fall to the ground. What happens?

## MORE FUN STUFF TO DO

Try the trick with other types of balls. Use a golf ball or a Ping-Pong ball in place of the tennis ball. Does the trick work the same way with all types of balls?

## EFFECT

When you drop the two balls at the same time, the tennis ball bounces very high, much higher than it bounced when you dropped it alone.

## EXPLANATION

When the you drop two balls, gravity pulls them to the ground. The basketball hits the ground first. The basketball begins to bounce up while the tennis ball is still falling down. As the basketball bounces up, it immediately hits the tennis ball. The force of the basketball moving up gives the tennis ball a greater bounce than its bounce would be if it had hit a flat surface.

## PROJECT 7 Comeback Can

*With this trick you can make it seem as if a can will return to you when you call it. Only it isn't really obeying you; it's obeying the laws of science!*

**Note: This activity requires adult help.**

## MATERIALS

hammer

2 nails

empty, clean coffee can with plastic lid

rubber band slightly longer than the coffee can

transparent tape

several weights (heavy nuts and bolts)

3-inch (7.5-cm) piece of string

adult helper

## THE SETUP

I. Ask an adult to use the hammer and one of the nails to punch a hole in the center of the bottom of the coffee can and a similar hole in the plastic lid.

2. Slip the rubber band through the hole in the bottom of the can from the inside, just enough so that a loop pops out of the bottom. Put the nail through the loop, and secure the nail to the outside of the can with tape.

3. Attach weights to the middle of the rubber band by tying the string tightly around both the weights and the rubber band.

4. Pull the free end of the rubber band through the hole in the plastic lid. The rubber band should be taut. Slip the other nail through the loop in the rubber band and secure the nail to the lid with tape. Snap the lid onto the can.

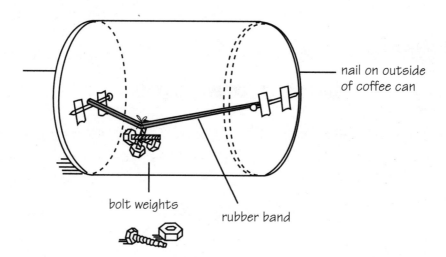

nail on outside of coffee can

bolt weights

rubber band

## MAGIC SCIENCE TIME!

1. Tell the audience that you have a magnetic hand.

2. Gently roll the can on a hard, smooth, flat surface. Just before the can stops rolling, hold your hand out and say some magic words commanding it to return.

## EFFECT

The can rolls away from you for a short distance, then it stops and rolls back to you.

# EXPLANATION

There are two main types of energy. **Kinetic energy** is the energy of moving objects. Potential energy is stored energy that has the ability to change into kinetic energy. Energy is never used up; it is just converted from one form or another. **Elastic energy** is a form of potential energy stored in a material when its shape is changed either by **stretching** (pulling apart) or **compressing** (pushing together). In this activity, elastic energy is stored in a stretched rubber band. The can converts that stored energy into kinetic energy.

When you give the Comeback Can a push, the forward movement of the can winds the rubber band, converting the kinetic energy of your push to stored elastic energy. When the kinetic energy given to the can by your push is used up, the can stops rolling. The stored energy in the rubber band then causes the band to unwind inside the can. The elastic energy in the rubber band is converted back to kinetic energy, and the can rolls back to you.

# The Magic of Electricity and Magnetism

## "Shocking" Illusions

**E**lectricity is a form of energy caused by the movement of one part of an atom called the electron. All matter is made up of atoms, and atoms are made up of even smaller particles called **protons**, **neutrons**, and **electrons**. An electron is the part of the an atom that orbits, or makes a circular path around the center of the atom called the **nucleus**. Electrons are capable of moving from one atom to another. This flow of electrons produces electricity.

The movement of electrons also causes magnetism. **Magnetism** is the invisible force that causes some substances to **attract** (come together) or **repel** (push apart) other substances.

Try the activities in this chapter to learn some tricks that might "shock" you!

## PROJECT

# Dancing Crispies

*Some cereals make alot of noise. Try this activity to see if you can make crispy rice cereal jump and dance, too.*

### MATERIALS

paper towel

1 teaspoon (5 ml) crispy rice cereal

balloon

wool sweater

### THE SETUP

1. Place the paper towel on the table.

2. Put the cereal on the paper towel.

### MAGIC SCIENCE TIME!

1. Tell the audience, "You have heard that crispy rice cereal snaps, crackles, and pops. I am now going to show you how to make it jump and dance."

2. Blow up the balloon and knot the end.

3. Rub the balloon several times on the wool sweater.

4. Bring the balloon near the cereal. Observe what happens.

# MORE FUN STUFF TO DO

Try this trick with other types of puffed cereal. Will it work with puffed wheat or puffed oats?

## EFFECT

The cereal is attracted to the balloon.

## EXPLANATION

This trick works because of **static electricity**, which is electricity that does not flow. Static electricity builds up with friction, which is created when two objects, such as wool and a balloon, rub together. All objects are made of atoms, and every atom has an equal number of protons and electrons. Protons have a positive charge and electrons have a negative charge. When these charges are equal, an object is neutral or uncharged. However, some objects, such as wool or hair, easily lose electrons. When you rubbed the balloon with the wool, some electrons moved from the wool to the balloon. The balloon then has a negative static charge.

When you bring the negatively charged balloon near the crispy cereal, the negatively charged balloon repels the electrons in each piece of cereal. The electrons move to the opposite side of the cereal. This gives the side of the cereal nearest the balloon a positive static charge and the piece of cereal is attracted to the negatively charged balloon.

Over a longer period of time, the electrons will transfer from the balloon to the cereal. Eventually, the balloon will become neutral and the cereal will fall back to the table.

**PROJECT**

# 2 Magic Compass

*There are many ways that a magician can make objects seem to move without touching them. Check out one way in this activity.*

## MATERIALS

glue

1-by-1-inch (2.5-by-2.5-cm) square piece of wood or wooden block

sewing needle

scissors

piece of typing paper

glass drinking glass (do not use plastic) with at least a 2-inch (5-cm) diameter (length of a line passing through the center of the circle formed by the rim of the glass)

wool sweater

## THE SETUP

1. Place a drop of glue in the center of the piece of wood.

2. Hold the eye end of the needle in the glue at a right angle (perpendicular) to the wood. Hold it steady until the glue dries enough so that the needle can stand by itself. Set the wood and needle aside until the glue dries completely.

3. Use the scissors to cut a piece of paper into a rectangle that measures ½-by-1½ inch (1.25-by-3.75 cm).

4. Fold the paper in half lengthwise. Open the paper and fold it again widthwise. Open the paper again. The place where the folds meet is the center of the paper.

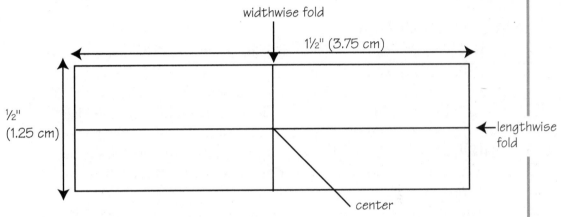

## MAGIC SCIENCE TIME!

1. Tell the audience, "I can create my own compass that will point to me rather than the North Pole."

2. Place the wood and needle on the table in front of you.

3. Balance the piece of paper on the needle by placing the center of the two folds on the point of the needle. Tell the audience, "This is my compass."

4. Place the glass over the entire setup. Tell the audience, "The glass will keep my breath from moving the paper compass."

5. Say a few magic words, telling the paper compass to obey your commands. Rub the wool on the side of the glass in a place that is farthest away from the ends of the paper. Watch what happens.

## MAGIC SCIENCE TRICK TIPS

This trick can also be done in another, more spectacular, way. Stick a coin on edge in a piece of plasticine. Balance a paper match on the top of the coin. Cover the setup with a glass or glass jar. Again rub the side of the glass with wool and watch what happens.

## EFFECT

The paper will turn and point to the place where you rub the glass with the wool.

## EXPLANATION

This trick also works because of static electricity. When you rub the glass with the wool, electrons rub off the wool and move onto the glass. A negative static charge builds up on the side of the glass where you rub. The negative charges in the glass repel the negative charges in the paper. The part of the paper closest to the glass becomes positively charged. The positively charged paper is attracted to the negatively charged glass. The paper turns toward the place where you rubbed the glass.

# PROJECT
# 3 Separation

*Can you separate a pile of salt and pepper? This activity shows you how.*

## MATERIALS

paper towel
1 teaspoon (5 ml) salt
1 teaspoon (5 ml) black pepper
spoon
balloon
wool sweater
helper

## THE SETUP

1. Place the paper towel on the table.

2. Put the salt and pepper on the paper towel.

## MAGIC SCIENCE TIME!

1. Ask a member of the audience to be your helper.

2. Mix the salt and pepper thoroughly with the spoon. Ask the helper to try to separate the grains of salt and pepper.

3. When the helper gives up trying to separate them, have him or her sit down.

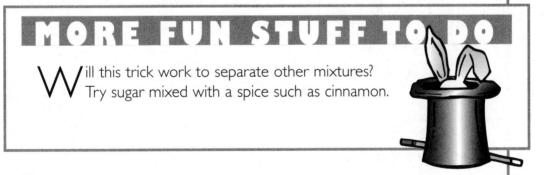

4. Blow up the balloon and tie the end in a knot. Rub the balloon on the wool sweater.

5. Bring the balloon near the salt-and-pepper mixture. What happens?

## MORE FUN STUFF TO DO

Will this trick work to separate other mixtures? Try sugar mixed with a spice such as cinnamon.

## EFFECT

The pepper is attracted to the balloon, but the salt is not.

## EXPLANATION

Again, this trick is an example of static electricity in action. When you rub the balloon with the wool cloth, the balloon becomes negatively charged. When you bring the balloon near the salt and pepper mixture, the pepper is attracted to the balloon. This is because electrons in the pepper move to the side of the pepper opposite the balloon. The side of the pepper near the balloon becomes positively charged. The positively charged part of the pepper is attracted to the negative charge on the balloon. The pepper sticks to the balloon.

The salt is not attracted to the balloon because the electrons in salt do not move easily. When you bring the balloon near the salt, the electrons in the salt stay where they are. The side of the salt near the balloon does not become charged—the salt remains uncharged or neutral. Thus the salt is not attracted to the negatively charged balloon.

## PROJECT 4

# Bending Water

*In the previous activities, you have used static electricity to make cereal dance and to separate pepper from salt. Try this activity to see how static electricity can make water move.*

## MATERIALS

sink with running tap water
balloon
wool sweater

## THE SETUP

Find a place to do this activity where you have access to running water. The kitchen would be a good place to perform this trick.

## MAGIC SCIENCE TIME!

1. Tell the audience, "I am going to use magic to make water move."

2. Turn on the tap and let the water run in a narrow stream.

3. Say a few magic words to make the water move. When this doesn't happen, tell your audience you need some help from your magic balloon and magic sweater.

4. Blow up the balloon and tie one end in a knot. Rub the balloon on the wool sweater.

5. Say a few more magic words, then bring the balloon near the stream of water. What happens?

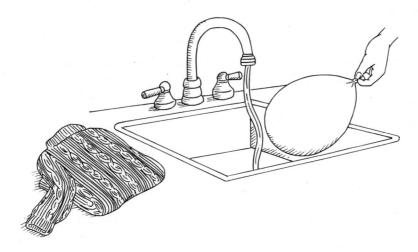

## EFFECT

The water moves toward the balloon.

## EXPLANATION

When you rub the balloon with the wool, electrons are transferred from the wool to the balloon and the balloon becomes negatively charged. The negative charge in the balloon causes some of the electrons in the water to move to the side of the water stream opposite to the balloon. The side of the water near the balloon becomes positively charged. The positively charged side of the water stream moves toward the negatively charged balloon.

The stream of water has to be small in order for movement to occur. The static charge on the balloon is relatively weak and cannot move large amounts of water.

If water touches the balloon, the balloon loses its static charge. The extra electrons move to the water, both the water and the balloon become electrically neutral, and the water no longer moves toward the balloon.

# PROJECT 5

# No Strings Attached

*Try this activity to learn how to make magnets float in the air—no strings attached!*

## MATERIALS

2 circular magnets with holes in the middle (available from science stores). The holes in the middle should be slightly larger than the diameter of the pencil.

felt-tip pen

pencil

## THE SETUP

1. Place the materials on the table in front of you.

2. Try to hold the flat parts of the magnets together until you find the two sides that repel. Mark those sides with the felt-tip pen so that you'll know how to place the magnets so that they repel.

## MAGIC SCIENCE TIME!

1. Tell the audience, "I am going to make a piece of metal float in the air."

2. Hold the pencil pointing up. Slip one of the magnets over the pencil, so that the pencil goes through the hole in the magnet.

3. Place the other magnet on the pencil so that the two magnets repel. Watch what happens.

## MAGIC SCIENCE TRICK TIPS

Try this with several magnets, so that each repels the one above it. This will make the trick look even more spectacular.

## EFFECT

The second magnet repels and floats above the first magnet.

## EXPLANATION

Every magnet is surrounded by a **magnetic field**—an invisible field of force. A magnet has a north pole and a south pole. North and south poles are attracted to each other, but a north pole will repel a north pole and a south pole will repel a south pole.

Magnets attract and repel because they are different from other solid objects. All matter is made of atoms and all atoms have electrons in orbit around their nucleus (center). Each electron, spinning in its orbit around the nucleus of the atom, creates a small magnetic field, called a **domain**. However, in magnets, the atoms are lined up so that they point in the same direction. If the atoms were large enough to see, they might look like thousands of spinning tops on a table. These lined-up atoms and their spinning electrons make an object a magnet. In nonmagnetic objects, the atoms are randomly arranged and their individual magnetic fields cancel each other out.

# PROJECT

# 6  Floating Needle

*Try this activity to make sewing needles float in the air.*

## MATERIALS

2 12-inch (30-cm) pieces of thread

2 sewing needles

transparent tape

1 quart (1 liter) clean, dry glass jar with lid

ruler

small flat magnet

## THE SETUP

1. Push one piece of thread through the eye of one of the needles. Pull the thread through the needle so that the needle is in the middle of the thread.

2. Fold the thread back on itself and knot the ends.

3. Tape the knotted end of the thread to the bottom of the jar. Use the ruler to make sure that when you extend the needle and thread, the tip of the needle reaches to about 1 inch (2.5 cm) from the mouth of the jar. If necessary, adjust the tape.

4. Repeat Steps 1 through 3 with the second needle and thread.

5. Make a reverse loop with a piece of tape so that the sticky side is on the outside. Stick the tape loop to the inside of the jar lid.

6. Stick the flat magnet to the tape and put the lid on the table.

7. Turn the jar upside down. Put on the lid and screw it on. The needles should be attracted to the magnet.

8. Turn the jar right side up. The needles should continue to be attracted to the magnet. If the magnet is not strong enough, lengthen the thread until the needles can be held upright by the magnetic field.

9. Unscrew the lid and place it on the table next to the jar.

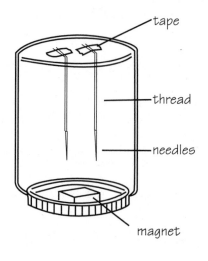

tape

thread

needles

magnet

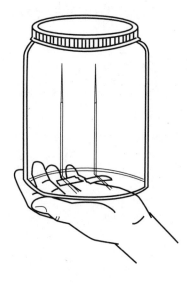

## MAGIC SCIENCE TIME!

1. Tell the audience, "I am going to make the needles in the jar rise up off the bottom of the jar. I have tied threads to them to make sure that they do not get away after I say the magic words."

2. Wave your hand over the jar and command the needles to rise. The needles will not move.

3. Tell the audience, "These must be Australian needles that have to be turned upside down to work."

4. Turn the jar upside down. Hold it over the lid and screw it in place. Again say a few magic words and command the needles to rise. The needles will be hanging down.

5. Tell the audience, "The needles have obeyed my command because in Australia, these needles would be right side up."

6. Your audience will think that the needles are just hanging down because of gravity so turn the jar right side up. The needles will remain in position.

## MAGIC SCIENCE TRICK TIPS

You can do this trick in another way. Use the tape loop to stick the magnet to the palm of one hand. Keep the magnet hidden from the audience. Tape the thread with the sewing needle attached to the table. Lift the needle with the finger of the hand that has the magnet until the thread is tight. Open your hand slowly so that the magnet attracts the needle and holds it in place, making the needle appear to float in the air above the table.

## EFFECT

The needles are extended on their strings and appear to be floating in air inside the jar.

## EXPLANATION

This trick works because of magnetism. The metal of the sewing needle is attracted to the magnet hidden in the lid of the jar. Only three metals are attracted to a magnet: iron, cobalt, and nickel. A sewing needle is made mainly of iron.

The magnet in this activity is a **permanent magnet**, meaning it keeps its magnetic power. But ordinary metal objects, such as the sewing needles, can become magnetized when they are put near a magnet.

# PROJECT 7
## The Disappearing Coin

*A magician can make things seem to disappear and then reappear somewhere else. This trick is an example.*

### MATERIALS
masking tape
paper cup
bar magnet
2 Canadian dimes minted in the same year (available from coin shops)
any 5 to 10 United States coins
helper

### THE SETUP
1. Make a reverse loop with the tape so that the sticky side is on the outside.
2. Stick the tape to the bottom of the paper cup. Stick the magnet to the tape.
3. Set the paper cup on the table. The audience should not be able to see the tape and magnet.
4. Place one Canadian dime in the cup. Tip the cup over to make sure that the magnet is strong enough to hold the coin in the cup. If the magnet is not strong enough, try other magnets until you find one that is strong enough. (Circular ceramic magnets, available from science stores, work well.)
5. Remove the Canadian dime from the cup. Place it on the table with the U.S. coins. Place the second Canadian dime in your pocket.

### MAGIC SCIENCE TIME!
1. Tell the audience, "I just got back from a trip to Canada. I liked

Canada, but I found that their coins acted strangely. They were very shy and would disappear from time to time, only to reappear later. Let me show you what I mean."

2. Ask a member of the audience to be your helper. Have the helper look at the pile of coins on the table and describe what he or she sees. The helper should tell the other audience members that there is only one Canadian coin and several U.S. coins.

3. Have the helper place the coins into the paper cup, but don't let him or her look inside.

4. Pick up the cup and shake the coins. Tell the audience, "The Canadian coin really hates to mingle. It will definitely disappear."

5. Dump the coins into the hands of your helper and say "Pick out the Canadian coin."

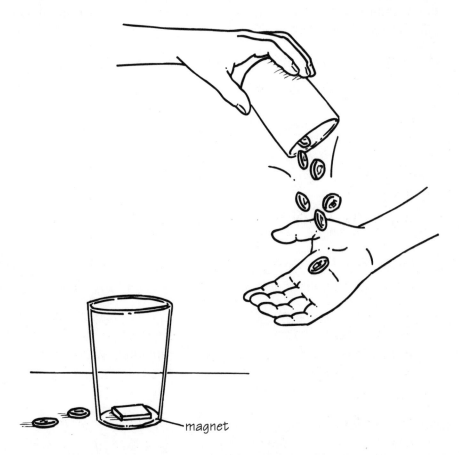

magnet

6. After the helper says that the coin cannot be found, pretend you hear the coin calling you from your pocket. Reach into your pocket and pull out the other Canadian dime.

## EFFECT

The audience thinks the Canadian coin vanished from the cup. The helper cannot find the Canadian coin among the coins you dumped into his or her hands. When you pull a duplicate coin out of your pocket, the audience will think that the coin reappeared in your pocket.

## EXPLANATION

This trick works because several Canadian coins: the dime, quarter, Loonie ($1 coin) and Twonie ($2 coin), are magnetic, while coins from the United States are not. This is because of the different metals they are made out of. When the coins are placed in the cup and shaken, the Canadian coin is attracted by the magnet in the bottom of the cup. When you pour out the coins, the coins from the United States pour out, but the Canadian coin remains stuck to the magnet on the bottom of the cup.

# Glossary

**absorb**  To take in.

**acid**  A type of chemical that reacts with a base to form a salt and water.

**air pressure**  The force exerted by the movement of air molecules.

**atom**  Tiny particles that make up matter.

**attract**  Cause to come together.

**base**  A type of chemical that reacts with an acid to form a salt and water.

**Bernoulli's principle**  A natural law that states that when any fluid, such as air, flows, its pressure decreases as its speed increases.

**Cartesian diver**  A device, named after Rene Descartes, a sixteenth-century French mathematician, in which an eyedropper moves up and down in a bottle because of changes in pressure.

**center of gravity**  The point where the effect of gravity on an object seems to be concentrated.

**centripetal force**  Any force that pulls an object inward toward the center of a circle.

**chemical**  Any substance that can change when combined with another substance.

**chemical indicator**  A chemical that changes color when mixed with acids or bases.

**chemical reaction**  A change in matter in which substances break apart to produce one or more new substances.

**chemistry**  The science that studies matter.

**colloid**  A mixture of tiny particles of one substance scattered evenly throughout another.

**compressing**  Pushing together.

**condense**  To change from a gas to a liquid.

**convection**  The process by which heat travels in moving currents through fluids (liquids and gases).

**density**  A physical property of matter used to compare two substances that have equal volumes but unequal masses.

**domain**  The small magnetic field created by electrons spinning in orbit around the nucleus of an atom.

**elastic energy** A form of potential energy stored in a material when its shape is changed.

**electricity** A form of energy caused by the movement of one part of an atom called the electron.

**electrons** The part of an atom that orbits, or makes a circular path around the center of the atom. It has a negative charge.

**element** A substance that cannot be further broken down chemically.

**evaporate** To change from a liquid to a gas.

**fluid** A substance that flows and can change shape easily.

**force** Something that changes the shape or movement of an object.

**friction** A force that opposes motion and slows down the movement of objects over each other.

**gravity** The force of attraction between two objects due to their mass.

**homogenized** To process milk in order to make the fat in it very fine and spread evenly throughout the milk.

**hygroscopic** Having the ability to easily absorb and hold water.

**hypothesis** An educated guess about the results of an experiment.

**inertia** The tendency of objects to resist a change in motion.

**kinetic energy** The energy of moving objects.

**law of inertia** An object at rest stays at rest, and an object in motion stays in motion, unless acted on by an outside force.

**lubricant** A filmlike substance that reduces friction.

**magnetic field** An invisible field of force.

**magnetism** The invisible force that causes some substances to attract (bring together) or repel (push apart) other substances.

**matter** Anything that has mass and occupies space.

**molecule** Atoms bonded or linked together.

**neutral** Neither an acid nor a base.

**neutralize** To mix together an acid and a base so that they cancel each other out.

**neutron** A part of an atom found in the nucleus. It has no electrical charge.

**normal** A line perpendicular to the surface, toward which light bends.

**nucleus** The center of an atom, made up of protons and neutrons.

**permanent magnet** A magnet that keeps its magnetic power.

**polar molecule** A particle (molecule) in which one end has a positive charge and the other end has a negative charge.

**polyethylene plastic** The plastic formed when ethylene molecules are joined together. It is used to make plastic bags.

**polymer** A long chain of molecules joined together with chemical bonds.

**potential energy** Stored energy.

**protons** A part of an atom found in the nucleus. It has a positive charge.

**refraction** The change in direction of light as it moves from one transparent substance to another.

**reflection** The bouncing of light from a surface.

**repel** Push apart.

**scientific method** A method of scientific investigation which begins with a hypothesis, then proceeds with an experiment, analysis of the results, and forming a conclusion.

**solution** One substance dissolved completely into another.

**static electricity** Electricity that does not flow.

**steam** The hot water vapor formed when water boils.

**stretching** Pulling apart.

**surface tension** The force of attraction between water molecules that creates a "thin skin" on the surface of the water.

**symmetrical** Exactly the same on both sides of the center.

**volume** The amount of space occupied by a substance.

**water pressure** The force per unit of area created by the continual sliding past one another and moving around of water molecules.

**water vapor** The gas form of water.

# Index